[redacted]

KNITTING ON THE ROAD

Sock Patterns for the Traveling Knitter

Nancy Bush

INTERWEAVE PRESS

Editor, Judith Durant
Technical editor, Dorothy T. Ratigan

Photography, Joe Coca
Cover and page design, Bren Frisch
Illustrations in Techniques section, Gayle Ford, Susan Strawn Bailey
Production, Dean Howes

Interweave Press
201 East Fourth Street
Loveland, CO 80537
USA
www.Interweave.com

Printed in Singapore

Library of Congress Cataloging-in-Publication

Bush, Nancy, 1951-
Knitting on the road: sock patterns for the traveling knitter / Nancy Bush.
p. cm.
ISBN 1-883010-91-8
1.Knitting—Patterns. 2. Socks. I.Title.

TT825.B89 2001
746.43'20432-dc21 2001024623

First printing: IWP-10M:401:TWP
Second printing: IWP-5M:1001:TWP
Third printing: IWP-5M:102:TWP

CONTENTS

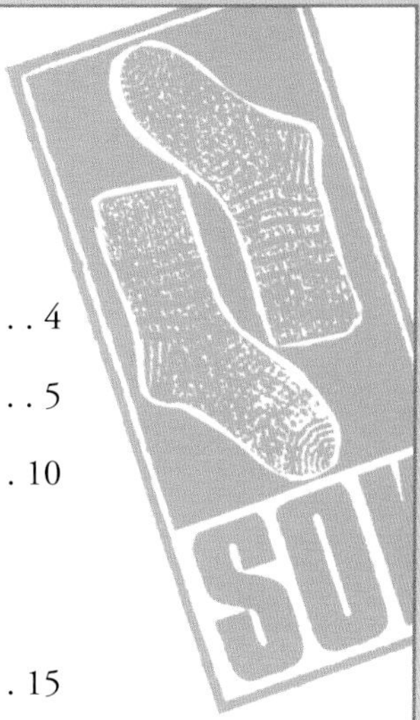

PATTERNS

INTRODUCTION

This book was inspired by journeys, by crowded airports and hotel rooms in faraway cities. I have always recommended that traveling knitters take along a small project, one worked on small needles with fine yarn. There's a lot of knitting, yet the materials don't fill a suitcase! Socks are great travelers' projects.

These socks were designed for knitting "on the go"—many of the patterns are "pretty easy." A few are more challenging, but the designs flow so that after a couple of repeats, you should be able to sail along with few glances at the text or graph. Some of the socks will be quick to knit, others will take more time; your knitting may fill that two-week vacation or only a six-hour layover.

The world offers lots of yarns for socks, and I've included an extensive list on pages 11–13. I knitted the socks with yarns I love or wanted to try and hope you will use this list to discover yarns you love as well.

While working on the patterns, I realized that even though I did most of the work at home, the process was a journey. I was transported to the places that inspired the designs; I could knit and dream of special events and memories, of scenes I saw, food I ate, and people I met. I remembered other knitting, done in other places, and discovered that knitting itself is a journey, a craft that will take you anywhere you want to go, as far as imagination will allow. Knitting is a connection to history, other cultures, and even make-believe. And so, included with these patterns comes a wish: "May you always have wonderful knitting journeys—wherever they take you!"

TECHNIQUES FOR KNITTING ON THE ROAD

GAUGE

Gauges in the sock patterns are based on knitting worked circularly, and you won't get an accurate gauge if you work back and forth. Always check gauge in the method called for in the pattern. Since socks don't (usually) take a lot of stitches to make a round (not like a sweater), I will start knitting the sock to get my gauge. If I am way off, well, ripping is part of the process. If I am right on or very close, I am ahead of the game, with some of the sock already knitted.

Here is a conversion chart that may help in choosing a substitue yarn. See also list of sock yarns on pages 11–13, which lists many sock yarns by length per weight.

ounces	=	grams × 0.035
grams	=	ounces × 28.57
yards	=	meters × 1.0936
meters	=	yards × 0.9144

50 g	=	1.75 ounces
100 g	=	3.50 ounces
1 ounce	=	28.57 grams
4 ounces	=	114.28 grams

10 yards	=	9.14 meters
10 meters	=	10.93 yards

CASTING ON

When knitting socks, I like to cast on over two needles held together as one in my right hand. This makes the cast-on stitches loose (but not sloppy) on the needle, which in turn makes the first round easier to work, and gives the cast-on edge a bit of stretch.

I have also become a passionate five-needle sock knitter and have written most of the patterns in this book for five needles—four to hold the stitches and the fifth to knit them. However, sometimes it's easier to work a pattern on four needles, especially when there is a pattern that runs down the front of a sock and continues down the instep. Those patterns have been written for four needles—three to hold the stitches and the fourth to knit them. If you want to knit one of my five-needle patterns on four needles, simply place the stitches I have on needles #2 and #3 (the instep stitches) together onto one needle. Place a marker between each group so you will know which stitches belong where. This is especially important when shaping heels and toes.

Continental Long-tail Cast-on

This method of casting on gives a firm yet elastic edge. Make a slip knot and place it on the right needle, leaving a long tail (the length of this tail will depend on how many stitches you need to cast on). Place the thumb and index finger of your left hand between the two threads. Secure the long ends by closing your other three fingers on them. Twist your wrist so that your palm faces upward and spread your thumb and index finger apart to make a **V** of the yarn around them.

Insert a needle into the loop of yarn around your thumb from front to back. Place the needle over the top of the yarn around your index finger and bring the needle down through the loop around your thumb. Drop the loop off your thumb and, placing your thumb back in the **V** configuration, tighten up the resulting stitch on the needle. Repeat this process until all stitches are cast on.

Continental Long-tail Cast-on

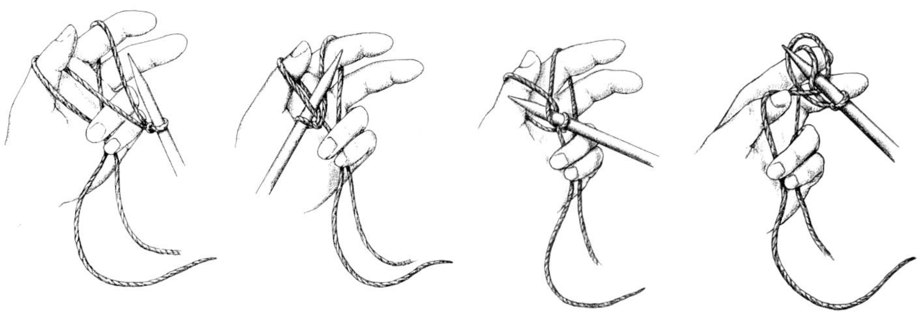

Long-tail Thumb Cast-on

This method of casting on gives a firm, yet elastic edge—the results are the same as for the Continental Long-tail Cast-on. This cast-on is knitted, using your left thumb as the left "needle."

Place a slipknot on the right needle, leaving a long tail (the length of this tail will depend on how many stitches you need to cast on). Wrap the tail end around your left thumb, clockwise. Hold the needle with the slipknot in your right hand and wrap the yarn from the ball over your right index finger. Insert the needle through the loop around your thumb from front to back. With your right index finger, wrap the yarn from the ball around the needle as if to knit (this is a counterclockwise wrap). Pull this yarn through the loop around your thumb to make a stitch. Tighten the resulting loop on the needle. Continue in this manner until you have the desired number of stitches cast on.

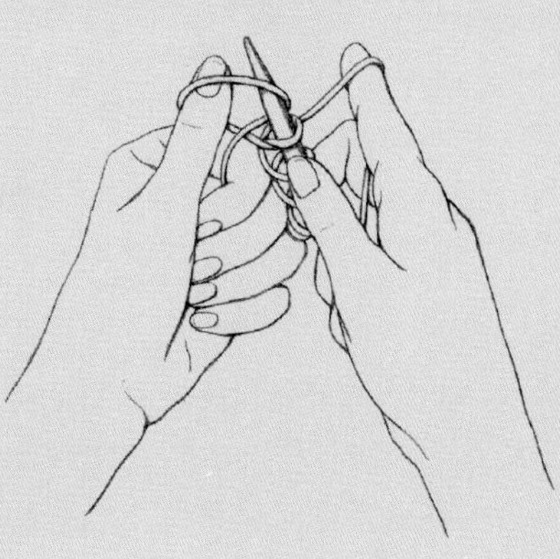

English Cast-on

This cast-on is worked in much the same way as the Continental Long-tail Cast-on, but there is an extra twist in the yarn. This twist secures the stitch, making the cast-on a bit stronger and also more decorative.

Make a slipknot and place it on the right needle, leaving a long tail (the length of this tail will depend on how many stitches you need to cast on). Place the thumb and index finger of your left hand between the two threads. Secure the long ends by closing your other three fingers on them. Twist your wrist so that your palm faces upward and spread your thumb and index finger apart to make a **V** of the yarn around them. Place the needle in front of the yarn around your thumb and bring it underneath both threads around your thumb (figure 1). Insert the needle down through the center of the loop around your thumb and bring the needle forward toward you (figure 2). The loop around your thumb will have a twist in it, close to the needle. Place the needle over the top of the yarn around your index finger, catch this yarn, and insert the needle back down into the loop around your thumb. As you do this, turn your thumb slightly away from you to remove the twist in the loop and allow the needle to pass through the untwisted loop. Drop the loop off your thumb and, placing your thumb back in the **V** configuration, tighten up the resulting stitch on the needle (figures 3 & 4). Repeat this process until all stitches are cast on.

English Cast-on

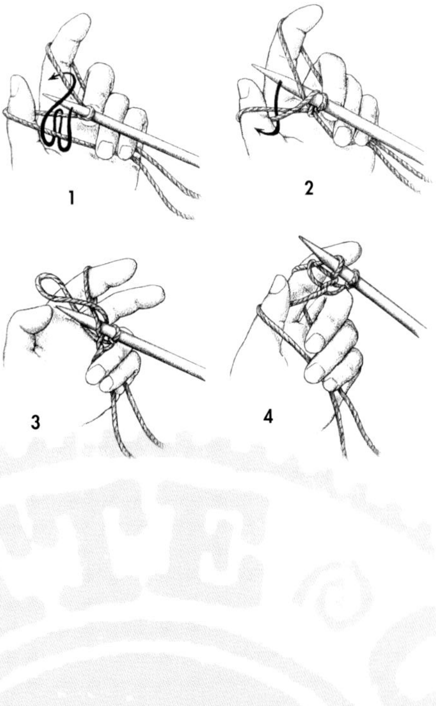

Double-start Cast-on

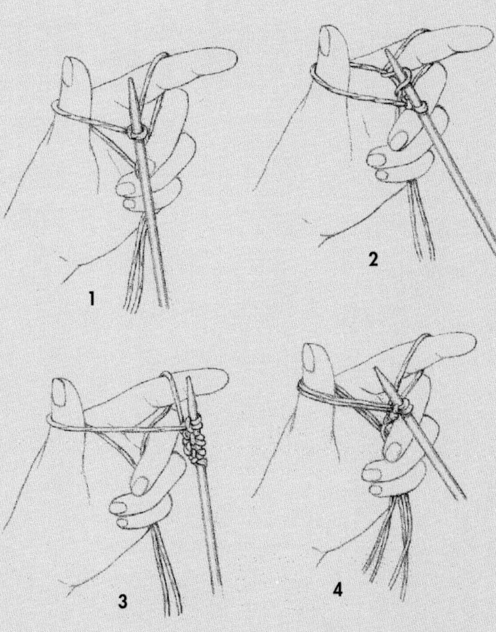

This cast-on is a variation of the Continental Long-tail Cast-on. It makes a decorative edge and can be worked with one, two, or three strands around the thumb.

The two parts (A and B) worked one after the other result in a double thread running in front of two cast-on stitches. Part B by itself results in a cast-on edge like the Continental Long-tail Cast-on, but the front of the stitches will angle to the left rather than to the right.

Make a slipknot and place it on the right needle, leaving a long tail (the length of this tail will depend on how many stitches you need to cast on). To begin, the slipknot will be considered Part A of the cast-on. Place the thumb and index finger of your left hand between the two threads. Secure the long ends by closing your other three fingers on them. Twist your wrist so that your palm faces upward and spread your thumb and index finger apart to make a **V** of the yarn around them. This is the same as a Continental Long-tail Cast-on.

Release the yarn around your thumb and re-wrap it in the opposite direction from above (figure 1). With the needle, go straight down and catch the thread behind the thumb, go over the thread around the index finger, then bring the needle back through the thumb loop (figure 2). Drop the loop off your thumb and, placing your thumb back in the original **V** formation, tighten up the resulting stitch on the needle. This maneuver will be referred to as Part B. You have completed the first pair. Continue to cast on in pairs of stitches, with one Continental Long-tail Cast-on, (Part A) followed by one Part B (figure 3).

To cast on with a double yarn, measure a length of yarn for the number of stitches required, double this length, and fold the yarn. Make a slipknot about six inches in from the short tail at the end of the yarn opposite the loop—the slipknot is made in doubled yarn and will count as the first two stitches. When you begin the cast-on, place the doubled yarn around your thumb and the single strand around your index finger (figure 4). The short end will be woven in later. Cast on with Part A and Part B as described above.

JOINING STITCHES INTO A ROUND

I use the Cross-over Join, my favorite, in most circular knitting. You are free to use the join of your choice.

Cross-over Join

After you have cast on the necessary number of stitches and divided them evenly onto double pointed needles, slip the first stitch you cast on (at the point of the left needle) onto the right needle. With the left needle, pick up the last stitch cast on, which is now one stitch in from the end of the right needle, and bring it up over the top of the previously moved stitch, placing it onto the left needle. In essence, you have changed places with the first and the last cast-on stitches, and the second stitch moved (the last stitch cast on) surrounds the first.

Extra Stitch Join

Cast on one more stitch than necessary. Slip this extra stitch onto the left needle, placing it next to the first cast-on stitch and knit these two stitches together. This will give you the correct stitch count and also tidy up the joining place.

Two-end Join

Another good way to join your stitches is to work the first two or three stitches of the round with both ends of yarn. In other words, use the yarn attached to the ball and the tail that remains from casting on to work these stitches. After you have joined and worked several stitches in your chosen pattern, drop the tail end and continue on with the yarn attached to the ball. Remember that these first few stitches are doubled on the next round; work them as single stitches.

DECREASES

Right Slanting Decreases
K2tog (on RS)–knit two stitches together.
P2tog (on WS)–purl two stitches together.

Left Slanting Decreases
When stitches are slipped for a decrease, always slip as to knit.

Ssk (slip, slip, knit)–slip one stitch knitwise, slip one stitch knitwise, insert left needle into the front of the two slipped stitches from left to right and knit them together.

Sl 1, k1, psso (slip one, knit one, pass slipped stitch over)–slip one stitch knitwise, knit one, insert left needle into the front of the slipped stitch from left to right, lift the stitch, pass it over the knitted stitch, and drop it off the needle.

K2tog tbl (knit two together through the back loop)–knit two stitches together going into the back of the loops rather than the front of the loops.

HEEL TURNS

The two most common heel turns are what I call the Round Heel and the Square Heel. Both are done with short rows and both are sturdy.

Round Heel

This heel works best with an even number of stitches in the heel flap. Begin by knitting half way across the completed flap **to the middle**. If you have a flap with 34 stitches, knit 17. **Knit two more stitches**, work a left slanting decrease (see above), k1, turn. For the next row, sl 1, p5, p2tog, p1, turn. On the next row, sl 1, knit to within one stitch of the gap that was created on the first row. Work a left slanting decrease (the same one you used last time) to close the gap, k1, turn. On the next row, sl 1, purl to within one stitch of the gap, close this gap with a p2tog, p1, turn.

Repeat these last two rows until you have used up all the heel stitches. You will notice that after completing each purl-side row, you will have the same number of stitches after the gap on both sides and that these stitches reduce by two every time you complete a row. Also, depending on the number of stitches you start with, you might not have the k1 and p1 after the decrease on the last two rows. Don't fret, just carry on and complete the row.

When worked over the same number of stitches, the Round Heel leaves more stitches than the Square Heel. This means that you will have more stitches to decrease to get to the right number for the foot, resulting in a longer gusset.

Square Heel

This is worked in a similar manner to the round heel, but the result is quite different. This heel shaping can be worked over an even or an odd number of stitches. First you need to decide how many stitches you want in the middle third of the heel. If you have a number of stitches in the flap that is divisible by three, such as thirty, you will put ten stitches in the center and ten on each edge. To turn a heel with thirty stitches, knit across the first ten stitches of the flap and then knit across the next nine. Work the tenth stitch of this middle group together with the first stitch of the third group, using a left slanting decrease. Turn the work. Sl 1, p8 (the eight stitches exactly in the middle, the center part of the group of ten middle sts), p2tog, (this is the first stitch of the middle ten purled together with the last of the first ten). Turn work. Sl 1, k8, make a left slanting decrease. Turn work. Sl 1, p8, p2tog. Turn work. Repeat these last two rows until you have used up all the stitches at the edge. There are ten stitches remaining.

If your heel flap is not divisible by three, you have to decide where to put the odd number. For instance, if you have thirty-seven stitches in your heel flap, you may divide them so you have thirteen in the first third, eleven in the second, and thirteen in the last. The first and last third should always have the same number of stitches. Or you may divide them so you have twelve, thirteen, and twelve, thus having more stitches in the center. These center stitches will be added to the stitches you pick up from the sides of the heel flap to form the stitches on needles #1 and #4, and it is generally these stitches that remain after the heel is turned and are decreased when the gussets are shaped.

Making a Chain Stitch Edge on a Heel Flap

The edge of a heel flap should have one stitch (called a chain stitch) for every two rows of the flap. There are two ways to do this. The most common method is to slip the first stitch purlwise at the beginning of every row. Another way is to slip the last stitch of every row with the yarn in front and knit the first stitch of every row through the back loop. I use the first method, but you may choose the method you prefer.

Picking Up Chain Stitches and Shaping Gussets

To join the heel with the instep, you'll need to pick up the chain stitches. You'll begin at the heel, pick up stitches along the right side of the heel flap, work the instep stitches, then pick up stitches along the left side of the heel flap. "Right" and "left" refer to the sides of the heel flap when it is right side up, as though it was on your foot.

Here are two methods of picking up chain stitches. Use whichever method you prefer.

The most common way to pick up chain stitches is to go into the whole stitch at the edge and knit it.

Pick up and knit a whole chain stitch

If you pick up the front half of the chain stitches and knit through the back loop, the stitches will be tighter and there will be no gaps that may otherwise appear along the sides of the flap.

Pick up half a chain stitch . . .

. . . and knit it through the back loop

When picking up stitches for heel gussets, a hole may develop where the gusset meets the instep stitches. To avoid this problem, pick up one extra stitch between the last chain stitch of the heel flap and the beginning of the instep stitches. Place this extra stitch on the instep needle and work the instep. Before picking up the chain stitches on the other side of the heel flap, pick up one extra stitch and place it at the end of the instep needle. On the next round, ssk the first two stitches on the instep needle together and k2tog the last two stitches of the instep.

Kitchener Stitch

Use the kitchener stitch to join the remaining instep stitches to the remaining heel stitches after shaping a toe. You will need the same number of stitches on each needle. You may divide the stitches so that those from needles #1 and #4 are together on one needle and those from needles #2 and #3 are on the other needle. You may kitchener top to bottom or side to side.

Hold the two needles parallel. Thread your yarn onto a blunt point tapestry needle. If your yarn is coming from the right stitch on the back needle, begin by inserting the tapestry needle into the first stitch on the *front* needle as if to *knit* and slip this stitch off. Now go into the second stitch on the front needle as if to *purl* and leave this stitch on the needle. Insert the tapestry needle into the first stitch on the *back* needle as if to *purl* and slip this stitch off the needle. Now go into the second stitch on the back needle as if

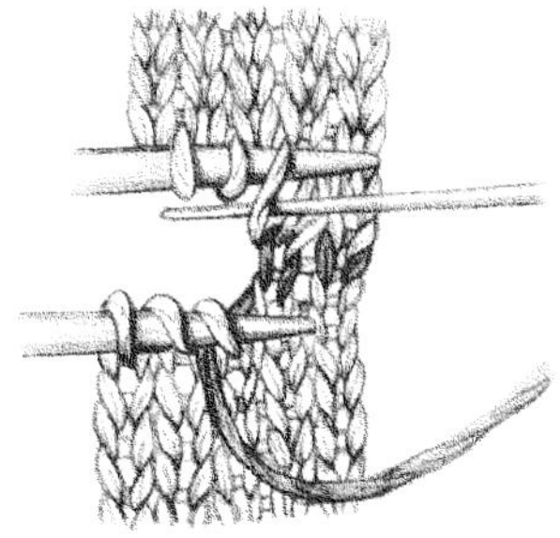

Kitchener stitch

to *knit* and leave this stitch on the needle. Repeat this process by going into the first stitch on the front needle (the one you left on the needle) as if to *knit* and slide it off the needle, then go into the second stitch on the front needle as if to *purl* and leave it on the needle. Now go into the first stitch on the back needle as if to *purl* and slide it off the needle, then go into next stitch on the back needle as if to *knit* and leave it on the needle. Work in this manner until all stitches are joined. Weave in the ends.

If your yarn is coming from the the front needle, go into the first stitch on the back needle as if to *purl* and slide it off the needle, then go into the next stitch as if to *knit* and leave it on the needle. Now take the tapestry needle into the first stitch on the front needle as if to *knit* and slide it off the needle, go into the next stitch as if to *purl* and leave it on the needle. Continue in this manner, alternating between front and back needles, until all stitches are joined.

ABBREVIATIONS

k	knit
p	purl
psso	pass slipped stitch over
p2sso	pass two slipped stitches over at the same time
sl 1	slip one stitch as if to purl unless otherwise stated
ssk	slip one stitch as if to knit, slip another stitch as if to knit, knit the two slipped stitches together.
st(s)	stitch(es)
tbl	through the back loop
tog	together
yo	yarn over

SOCK YARNS

The following list contains many yarns made especially for socks and available through yarn shops and by mail order and includes my favorites. I think it is important for knitters to be able to interchange yarns and not be tied to the same yarn a designer chooses.

This list offers the following information: yarn name and fiber content, yardage and meters, recommended stitch gauge, and recommended needle size. To find a yarn that will interchange with one called for in a pattern, the best place to start is with yardage and recommended stitch gauge. For example, let's say the yarn called for in the pattern is Wildfoote. It has 215 yards in 50 grams, knits at an average of 28 stitches to four inches on #1 or #2 needles and has a fiber content of 75% wool and 25% nylon. You don't happen to have any of this yarn in your stash, but you do have some Shepherd Sock Yarn. This yarn also has 215 yards in 50 grams, works at an average of 28 stitches to four inches on #1 or #2 needles and has the same fiber content. It is very likely (but not always a "sure thing") that these two yarns are interchangeable. The best way to know for sure is to knit a gauge swatch.

That being said, it is also possible to choose a substitute for a yarn where the two yarns have different amounts of yardage for the same weight, but knit at roughly the same gauge. An example here would be Shepherd Sock Yarn (215 yards in 50 grams and 28 stitches to four inches with needles #1 or #2) and St. Ives (198 yards in 50 grams and 28 stitches to four inches with needles #4). The yardage for these two yarns is different—the Shepherd Sock Yarn seems to be thinner than the St. Ives. However, they both have a recommended gauge of 28 stitches to four inches. The recommended needle size varies, but that doesn't matter. What's important is that you get the necessary gauge.

If you have a yarn that has a recommended stitch gauge that is close but not exactly what the pattern calls for, try changing the needle size, either up or down, to see if you can make your yarn choice work. You will run into trouble if you try to substitute a yarn that has 120 yards in 50 grams and knits at 24 stitches for four inches for a yarn that has 220 yards in 50 grams and knits at 32 stitches for four inches. The thicker yarn will not likely give you the gauge that you need. The thinner yarn may give you a gauge of 24 stitches to four inches, but the knitting will be so loose and sloppy that you probably won't like the result.

You may use many of these yarns at gauges other than those offered. The yarns are listed in order of length per weight, from the finest to the thickest.

Yarn name (content)	yards (meters)	weight	sts per 4" (10 cm)	needles
Kroy 3 ply (85% wool, 15% nylon)	262 (240)	50 g	32	#3 (3.25 mm)
Regia Cotton 4 ply (85% wool, 15% nylon)	248 (227)	50 g	30	#3 (3.25 mm)
Socka Cotton (32% wool, 53% cotton, 15% nylon)	238 (220)	50 g	31	#0–1 (2–2.25 mm)
Opal (75% wool, 25% polymide)	465 (425)	100 g	28	#1–2 (2.25–2.75 mm)
Happy Strumph (75% wool, 25% nylon)	231 (210)	50 g	28	#3 (3.25 mm)
Regia (75% wool, 25% acrylic)	231 (210)	50 g	30	#3 (3.25 mm)
Fortissima (75% wool, 25% nylon)	231 (210)	50 g	28	#2–3 (2.75–3.25 mm)
Fortissima Colori (75% wool, 25% nylon)	231 (210)	50 g	28	#2–3 (2.75–3.25 mm)
Fortissima Cotton (75% cotton, 25% nylon)	231 (210)	50 g	26	#1–2 (2.25 -2.75 mm)
Fortissima Cotolana (38% wool, 37% cotton, 25% nylon)	231 (210)	50 g	28	#2–3 (2.75–3.25 mm)
Fortissima Jeans (75% wool, 25% nylon)	231 (210)	50 g	28	#2–3 (2.75–3.25 mm)
Trekking (75% wool, 25% nylon)	231 (210)	50 g	28	#2–3 (2.75–3.25 mm)
Trekking Sport (75% wool, 25% nylon)	231 (210)	50 g	28	#2–3 (2.75–3.25 mm)
Trekking Tweed (75% wool, 25% nylon)	231 (210)	50 g	28	#2–3 (2.75–3.25 mm)
Trekking Stripe (75% wool, 25% nylon)	231 (210)	50 g	28	#2–3 (2.75–3.25 mm)
Aktif (75% wool, 25% nylon)	229 (210)	50 g	30	#2–3 (2.75–3.25 mm)
Special Blauband (80% wool, 20% nylon [5 g reinforcing thread included])	225 (210)	50 g	28	#3 (3.25 mm)
Special Multicolor (80% wool, 20% nylon [5 g reinforcing thread included])	225 (210)	50 g	28	#3 (3.25 mm)
Gems 6/3 (100% wool)	225 (210)	100 g	24	#4–5 (3.5–3.75 mm)
Socka 50 (75% wool, 25% nylon)	222 (205)	50 g	30	#1–2 (2.25–2.75 mm)
Socka Color (75% wool, 25% nylon)	222 (205)	50 g	30	#1–2 (2.25–2.75 mm)
Wildfoote (75% washable wool, 25% nylon)	215 (196)	50 g	28	#1–2 (2.25–2.75 mm)
Shepherd Sock Yarn (75% wool, 25% nylon)	215 (196)	50 g	28	#1–2 (2.25–2.75 mm)
JaWoll (75% wool, 18% nylon, 7% acrylic [5 g reinforcing thread included])	206 (190)	45 g	30	#1–2 (2.25–2.75 mm)
Kroy 4 ply (80% wool, 20% nylon)	203 (186)	50 g	28	#3 (3.25 mm)
Argyle (80% merino wool, 20% nylon)	197 (180)	50 g	28	#2–3 (2.75–3.25 mm)

Yarn name (content)	yards (meters)	weight	sts per 4" (10 cm)	needles
St. Ives (80% wool, 20% nylon)	198 (182)	50 g	28	#4 (3.5 mm)
Naturespun 3 ply Sport (75% wool, 25% nylon)	184 (168)	50 g	24	#5–6 (3.75–4 mm)
Sockenwolle (20% wool, 20% nylon, 60% acrylic)	180 (165)	50 g	24	#2–3 (2.75–3.25 mm)
Weaver's Wool Quarters (100% wool)	350 (320)	4 oz	26	#2 (2.75 mm)
Satakieli (100% wool)	360 (330)	100 g	28	#1–2 (2.25–2.75 mm)
Koigu Merino (100% merino wool)	176 (160)	50 g	24	#3 (3.25 mm)
Soft Touch Ultra (70% wool, 30% nylon)	175 (160)	50 g	28	#1–2 (2.25–2.75 mm)
Libero Mouline (75% wool, 25% nylon)	165 (150)	50 g	22	#3–5 (3.35–3.75 mm)
Libero Highland Tweed (75% wool, 25% nylon)	165 (150)	50 g	22	#3–5 (3.35–3.75 mm)
Strapaz (80% wool, 20% nylon)	164 (150)	50 g	25	#3–4 (3.25–3.5 mm)
Gjestal Silja Sock Yarn (80% wool, 20% nylon)	164 (150)	50 g	26	#4 (3.5 mm)
Fortissima 6 ply (75% wool, 25% nylon)	138 (126)	50 g	24	#3–4 (3.25–3.5 mm)
Socka 6-fach (75% wool, 25% nylon)	135 (125)	50 g	22	#5 (3.75 mm)
Happy Trails Sock Yarn (90% wool, 10% nylon)	132 (120)	50 g	24	#3 (3.25 mm)
Sedrun (90% wool, 10% nylon)	132 (120)	50 g	23	#5 (3.75 mm)
Tiur (90% wool, 10% nylon)	126 (115)	50 g	24	#3–4 (3.25–3.5 mm)
Guernsey 5 ply (100% wool)	245 (224)	100 g	28	#1–3 (2.25–3.25 mm)
Heilo (100% wool)	109 (100)	50 g	24	#3–4 (3.25–3.5 mm)
Viking Raggsokkegarn (80% wool, 20% nylon)	109 (100)	50 g	24	#1–3 (2.25–3.25 mm)
Country Classic (80% wool, 20% nylon)	215 (196)	4 oz	17	#8 (5 mm)
Peer Gynt (100% wool)	100 (91)	50g	22	#6 (4 mm)
Big Print (100% wool)	92 (85)	50 g	19	#6–8 (4–5 mm)
Big Socks (100% wool)	92 (85)	50 g	19	#6–8 (4–5 mm)
Big (100% wool)	92 (85)	50 g	19	#6–8 (4–5 mm)
Sockenwolle Plus (20% wool, 20% nylon, 60% acrylic)	90 (83)	50 g	17	#6–8 (4–5 mm)

Alphabetical by Manufacturer/Distributor

Accessories Unlimited
Country Classic

Aurora
Viking Raggsokkegarn

Berocco
St. Ives
Guernsey 5 ply
JaWoll

Brown Sheep Company
Naturespun 3 ply Sport
Wildfoote

Dale of Norway
Heilo
Tiur

Knitting Fever
Regia
Regia Cotton 4 ply

Koigu
Koigu Merino

Lorna's Laces
Shepherd Sock Yarn

Louet
Gems 6/3

Mountain Colors
Weaver's Wool Quarters

Muench
Aktif
Happy Strumph
Sockenwolle
Sockenwolle Plus
Strapaz

Newman Promotions
Opal

Patons
Kroy 3 ply
Kroy 4 ply

Plymouth
Gjestal Silja Sock Yarn

Russi Sales
Argyle

Shelridge Farms
Soft Touch Ultra

Skacel
Fortissima
Fortissima 100
Fortissima Colori
Fortissima Colori 100
Fortissima Cotolana
Fortissima Cotton
Fortissima Jeans
Fortissima 6 ply
Libero Highland Tweed
Libero Mouline
Trekking
Trekking Sport
Trekking Stripe
Trekking Tweed

Swedish Yarn Imports
Peer Gynt

Tahki/Stacy Charles
Big
Big Print
Big Socks
Socka Color
Socka Cotton
Socka 50
Socka 6-fach

Wheelsmith
Special Blauband
Special Multicolor
Sedrun

The Wooly West
Happy Trails Sock Yarn
Satakieli (retail only)

STRUMPF
SOK
ZOKNI
CHAUSSETTE

CANADA

The inspiration for these colorful socks comes from wonderful memories of my many visits to Canada and the delightful friendships I've formed with people who live there. The yarn is Canadian, from Shelridge Farms in Ontario, and the colors reflect a Canadian autumn. The technique for the "Latvian twist" was taught to me by Lucy Neatby, a very skilled British knitter, designer, and teacher who lives in Nova Scotia, and the main pattern is an Estonian design called "Maple Leaf." So many people have found refuge in this country, I like to think these socks reflect some of the diversity of cultures that are at home in Canada.

YARN

Shelridge Farms (100% Merino wool, 175 yd [160 m]/50 g): Forest (MC), 2 skeins; Cardinal (CC1) and Nutmeg (CC2), 1 skein each.

NEEDLES

Set of five double-pointed needles size 0 (2 mm) or size needed to obtain correct gauge.

GAUGE

16 sts and 22 rounds = 2 inches (5 cm) in circular stockinette stitch before blocking.

FINISHED SIZE

About 8¼ inches (21 cm) around foot and 9 inches (23 cm) from top of leg to bottom of heel.

TIP

To work the "Latvian" twist that starts this sock, it may be easier to work on regular straight needles that are longer than your double-pointed needles. Use the same size needles you will use for the sock, and cast all stitches onto one needle. Work back and forth on the longer needles until you have completed the twist, then transfer the stitches to four double-pointed needles and join into a round.

LEG

With CC2, cast on 72 sts. *Do not join into a round.* Leaving sts on one needle, attach MC and knit 2 rows (see Tip at left).

Attach CC1 and knit 2 rows. With MC, *k4, twist the remaining sts by rotating the left needle counterclockwise one full turn; repeat from * to end of row, end k4. Cut CC1 and CC2. Divide sts evenly onto 4 needles (18 sts on each needle) and join into a round. This join is the "seam" line and marks the beginning of all future rounds.

Rib: *K2, p2; repeat from *. Repeat this round 5 times total.

Join CC2. Change to stockinette stitch, follow chart 1, and work 5 rounds. Cut CC2. With MC, knit 1 round, purl 1 round, decreasing 2 sts on the purl round (p2tog at end of needle #1 and at beginning of needle #4). 70 sts remain (17 sts on needles #1 and #4 and 18 sts on needles #2 and #3).

Work Maple Leaf Pattern

Join CC1 and follow chart 2 for pattern. When chart is complete, cut CC1. With MC, knit 1 round, purl 1 round, decreasing 2 sts on the purl round (p2tog at beginning of needle #2 and at end of needle #3). 68 sts remain (17 sts on each needle).

Continue in stockinette stitch with MC, begin clock pattern as indicated on chart 3 over the last 3 sts on needle #1 and first 3 sts on needle #2, and the last 3 sts on needle #3 and the first 3 sts on needle #4, and work until leg measures 8 inches (20.5 cm) or desired length to top of heel. End ready to begin needle #4 of Round 1—last 17 sts of round.

HEEL

Heel Flap

Begin with first st on needle #4. *Sl 1, k1; repeat from * to end of needle #1, turn. P34, turn. These 34 sts form the heel flap. The remaining 34 sts will be held for the instep.

Row 1: *Sl 1, k1; repeat from *.

Row 2: Sl 1, p33.

Repeat the last 2 rows 16 more times for a total of 17 chain sts (see page 9) at each edge of heel flap.

Turn Heel

Row 1: (Sl 1, k1) over 17 sts, k2, ssk, k1, turn.

Row 2: Sl 1, p5, p2tog, p1, turn.

Row 3: Sl 1, knit to within one st of the gap, ssk, k1, turn.

Row 4: Sl 1, purl to within one st of the gap, p2tog, p1, turn.

Repeat Rows 3 and 4 until all heel sts are worked. There are 20 heel sts.

Heel Gussets

Knit 20 heel sts, pick up and knit 17 chain sts along

right side of heel flap. Work 34 instep sts beginning with Round 2 of clock pattern. With an empty needle, pick up and knit 17 chain sts along left side of heel flap, knit 10 sts from heel needle. There are 27 sts on needles #1 and #4, 17 sts on needles #2 and #3.

Round 1: Work to 3 sts from end of needle #1, k2tog, k1. Work instep sts in established pattern. K1, ssk at beginning of needle #4, work to end.

Round 2: Work even in established pattern.

Repeat the last 2 rounds until there are 17 sts on needles #1 and #4. 68 sts total.

FOOT

Continue even in established pattern until clock pattern measures 2½ inches (6.5 cm) beyond the last gusset decrease. Discontinue clock pattern and continue in stockinette stitch for ½ inch (1.3 cm).

Shape Toe

Round 1: *Work to last 2 sts on needle, k2tog; repeat from * to end of round.

Round 2: Work even.

Repeat the last 2 rounds until there are 8 sts on each needle. Work Round 1 (the decrease round) only until there are 8 sts remaining, 2 sts on each needle. Break yarn, thread tail through remaining sts, pull snug, and fasten off.

FINISHING

Weave in all ends. Block under a damp towel or on sock blockers.

forest (MC) | cardinal (CC1) | nutmeg (CC2) | purl

Chart 3

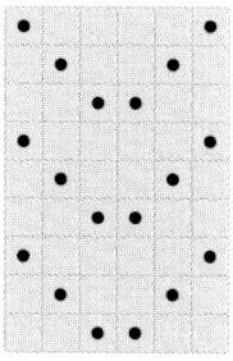

Chart 2

Repeat

Chart 1

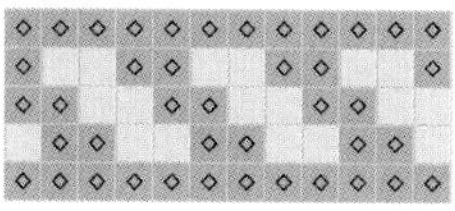

Repeat

CANAL DU MIDI

The inspiration for these socks came from one of the only true vacations I have had as an adult. Joe and I rented a narrow barge and spent a glorious week languishing on the Canal du Midi in southwest France. We took our time, enjoyed the views of vineyards, the cuisine, and the quiet. Needless to say, this was the perfect place to do some knitting! The pattern, which zigzags down the leg and foot of the sock, reminds me of our journey, stopping here and there to sample the life.

YARN

Satakieli (100% wool, 350 yd [320 m]/100 g): #132 Pale Yellow, 2 skeins.

NEEDLES

Set of five double-pointed needles size 0 (2 mm) or size needed to obtain correct gauge.

GAUGE

17 sts and 22 rounds = 2 inches (5 cm) in circular stockinette stitch before blocking.

FINISHED SIZE

About 7¾ inches (19.5 cm) around foot and 8¾ inches (22 cm) from top of leg to bottom of heel.

STITCHES

***Right Cross* K2tog and leave on needle, knit first st again, slip both sts off needle.**

***Left Cross* Knit second st through the back loop (tbl), knit first st, slip both sts off needle.**

LEG

Cast on 72 sts using a Double Start Cast-on with the strand over the thumb doubled (see page 7). Divide sts onto 3 needles (19 sts on needles #1 and #2, 34 sts on needle #3). Join into a round, being careful not to twist sts. This join is the "seam" line and marks the beginning of all future rounds. The seam line is at the side of the leg, not the center back.

Rib: *K2, p2; repeat from *. Repeat this round 5 times total. Follow chart as indicated, working rib as established over the first 38 sts (needles #1 and #2) and traveling stitch pattern over last 34 sts (needle #3).

Continue in established patterns until leg measures 4½ inches (11.5 cm), end having completed Round 6 of traveling stitch pattern.

Work 2 more repeats of the traveling stitch pattern, working stockinette stitch over first 38 sts (needles #1 and #2) and continuing pattern as established on needle #3.

First Decrease Round: Knit the first 2 sts tog on needle #1, knit to end of needle; knit to last 2 sts on needle #2, ssk; work instep sts as established. 70 sts remain.

Continue in established patterns for 5 more rounds.

Second Decrease Round: Work decrease round as before. 68 sts remain.

Continue in established pattern until leg measures 7½ inches (19 cm) or desired length to top of heel. End having completed Round 6 of pattern.

HEEL

Heel Flap

Knit 17 sts on needle #1 and 17 sts on needle #2 onto one needle, turn. P34, turn. These 34 sts form the heel flap. The remaining 34 sts will be held for the instep.

Row 1: Sl 1, k33.

Row 2: Sl 1, p33.

Repeat the last 2 rows 16 more times for a total of 17 chain sts (see page 9) at each edge of heel flap.

Turn Heel

Row 1: Sl 1, k20, ssk, turn.

Row 2: Sl 1, p8, p2tog, turn.

Row 3: Sl 1, k8, ssk, turn.

Row 4: Sl 1, p8, p2tog, turn.

Repeat Rows 3 and 4 until all heel sts are worked. There are 10 heel sts.

Heel Gussets

Knit 10 heel sts, pick up and knit 17 chain sts along right side of heel flap. Work 34 instep sts in established pattern. With an empty needle, pick up and knit 17 chain sts along left side of heel flap, knit 5 sts from heel needle. There are 22 sts on needles #1 and #3, 34 sts on needle #2.

Round 1: Work to 3 sts from end of needle #1, k2tog, k1. Work instep sts in established pattern. K1, ssk at beginning of needle #3, work to end.

Round 2: Work even in established pattern.

Repeat the last 2 rounds until there are 17 sts on needles #1 and #3. 68 sts total.

FOOT

Continue even in established pattern until foot measures 2½ inches (6.5 cm) less than desired finished length and you have completed Round 1 of traveling stitch pattern. Adjust sts onto four needles, 17 sts on each needle. Continue in stockinette stitch for ½ inch (1.3 cm).

Shape Toe

Round 1: *Ssk the first 2 sts on needle, knit to end of needle; repeat from *.

Round 2: Work even.

Repeat the last 2 rounds until there are 8 sts on each needle. Work Round 1 (the decrease round) only until there are 8 sts remaining, 2 sts on each needle. Break yarn, thread tail through remaining sts, pull snug, and fasten off.

FINISHING

Weave in all ends. Block under a damp towel or on sock blockers.

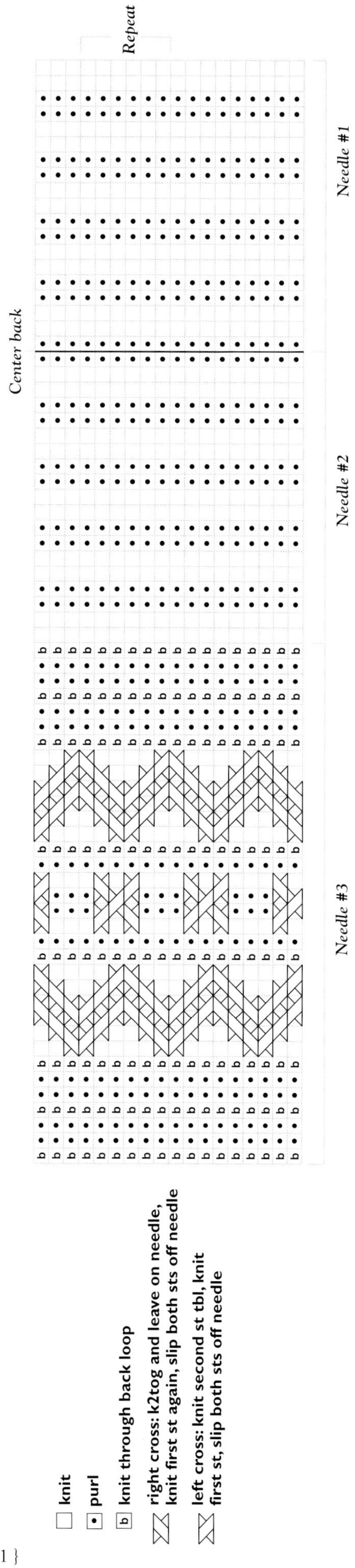

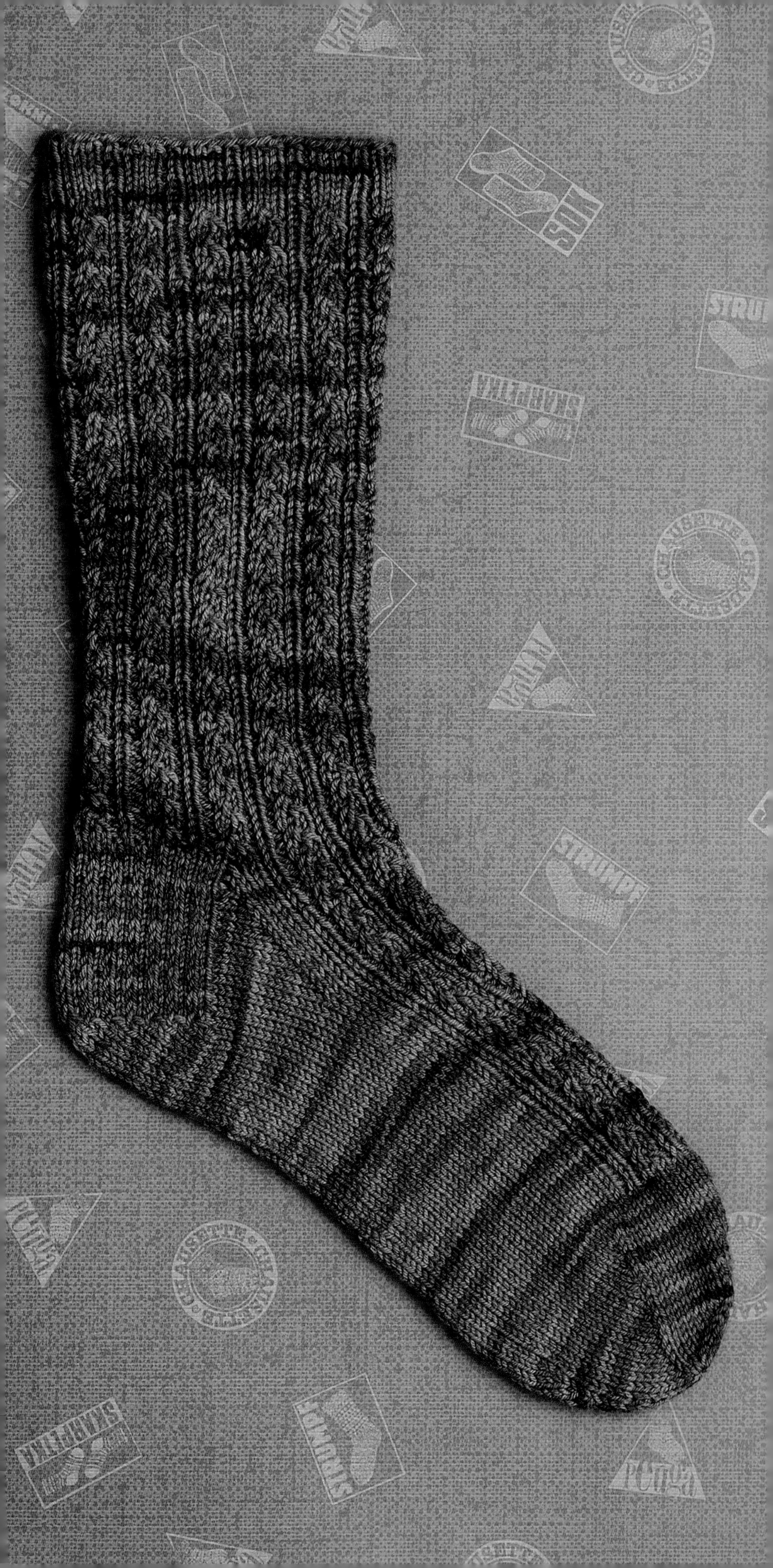
STRUMPF

CONWY

These interesting socks are named after a town in Gwynedd, the medieval kingdom of Owain Glyndwr, in Northern Wales. Walking along the old city wall with a view to the sea, I could imagine the dramatic history that had passed this way. Wales, especially Gwynedd, has a long tradition of sock knitting. The women would knit socks by the fireside and walk miles to sell their wares in the market towns. Time spent trekking through the hills nearby, visiting castles with towers and dungeons, viewing the landscape from the heights of Mt. Snowden, and coming upon a small woolen mill or two, made visiting this country very special.

YARN

Lorna's Laces Shepherd Sock Yarn (75% wool, 25% nylon, 215 yd [197 m]/50 g): #46 Jeans, 2 skeins.

NEEDLES

Set of five double-pointed needles size 1 (2.25 mm) or size needed to obtain correct gauge.

GAUGE

15 sts and 21 rounds = 2 inches (5 cm) in circular stockinette stitch before blocking.

FINISHED SIZE

About 7 inches (18 cm) around foot and 9½ inches (24 cm) from top of leg to bottom of heel.

TWINING CABLE PATTERN

Round 1: ***K1, p1, knit into second st on left needle, knit first st, slip both sts off needle, k1, p1; repeat from * to end.**

Round 2: ***K1, p1, k3, p1; repeat from * to end.**

Round 3: ***K1, p1, k1, knit into second st on left needle through the back loop (tbl), knit first st, slip both sts off needle, p1; repeat from * to end.**

Round 4: **Repeat Round 2.**

Repeat these 4 rounds for pattern.

LEG

Cast on 72 sts. Divide sts evenly onto 4 needles (18 sts on each needle) and join into a round, being careful not to twist sts. This join is the "seam" line and marks the beginning of all future rounds. *K1, p1, k3, p1, repeat from * to end. Work established ribbing pattern for 9 rounds total.

Begin Twining Cable Pattern and Shape Calf

Begin pattern as described at left and shown on chart, working 12 cables total, and *at the same time* on third repeat of Round 2 begin shaping decreases on needles #1 and #4 as indicated on chart. Repeat this decrease round every 8 rounds 5 more times—6 times total (three decrease rounds shown on chart). 60 sts remain.

Continue in established pattern until leg measures 8 inches (20.5 cm) or desired length to top of heel. End having completed Round 4 of pattern.

HEEL

Heel Flap

Knit 16 sts onto needle #1, turn. P31, turn. These 31 sts form the heel flap. The remaining 29 sts will be held for the instep.

Row 1: *Sl 1, k1; repeat from * ending last repeat k2.

Row 2: Sl 1, p30.

Repeat the last 2 rows 14 more times for a total of 15 chain sts (see page 9) at each edge of heel flap.

Turn Heel

Row 1: Sl 1, k15, ssk, k1, turn.

Row 2: Sl 1, p2, p2tog, p1, turn.

Row 3: Sl 1, knit to within one st of the gap, ssk, k1, turn.

Row 4: Sl 1, purl to within one st of the gap, p2tog, p1, turn.

Repeat Rows 3 and 4 until all heel sts are worked. There are 17 heel sts.

Heel Gussets

Knit 17 heel sts, pick up and knit 15 chain sts along right side of heel flap. Work 29 instep sts in established pattern beginning with Round 1 of Twining Cable pattern as follows: [k1, p1] 2 times, *knit into second st on left needle, knit first st, slip both sts off needle, k1, p1, k1, p1; repeat from * ending k1. With an empty needle, pick up and knit 15 chain sts along left side of heel flap, knit 8 sts from heel needle. There are 24 sts on needle #1, 14 sts on needle #2, 15 sts on needle #3, and 23 sts on needle #4.

Round 1: Work to 3 sts from end of needle #1, k2tog, k1. Work instep sts in established pattern. K1, ssk at beginning of needle #4, work to end.

Round 2: Work even in established pattern.

Repeat the last 2 rounds until there are 16 sts on needle #1 and 15 sts on needle #4. 60 sts total.

FOOT

Continue even in established pattern until foot measures 2 inches (5 cm) less than desired finished length. Discontinue Twining Cable pattern and continue in stockinette stitch.

Shape Toe

Place the last st on needle #1 onto needle #2. There are 15 sts on each needle.

Round 1: *Work to last 2 sts on needle, k2tog; repeat from *.

Round 2: Work even.

Repeat the last 2 rounds until there are 9 sts on each needle. Work Round 1 (the decrease round) only until there are 8 sts remaining, 2 sts on each needle. Break yarn, thread tail through remaining sts, pull snug, and fasten off.

FINISHING

Weave in all ends. Block under a damp towel or on sock blockers.

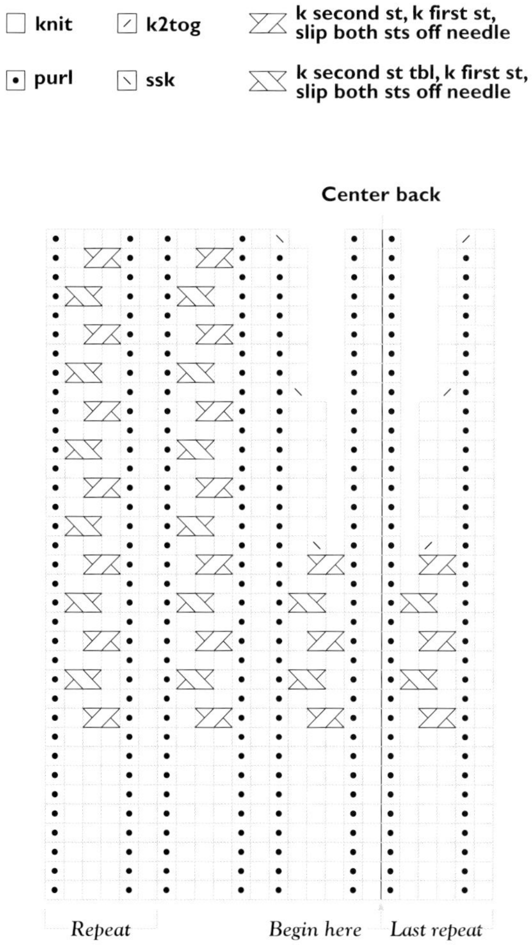

DALARNA

Dalarna, Sweden was the inspiration for these socks. This land is one of the most traditional in all of Sweden, and people carry on the old ways in everyday life—they work the fields and celebrate midsummer by decorating a tall pole with birch leaves and flowers. I went to weaving school in Dalarna and it is here that I *really* learned to knit. *Tvåändsticknin*g or twined knitting was historically popular throughout Dalarna, and it is still done there today. This design, while not entirely twined, uses a decorative chain as part of the pattern. I chose the color because red is the traditional color of ladies' stockings.

YARN

Wendy Guernsey (100% wool, 245 yd [224 m]/100 g): #590 Red, 2 skeins.

NEEDLES

Set of five double-pointed needles size 1 (2.25 mm) or size needed to obtain correct gauge.

GAUGE

14 sts and 21 rounds = 2 inches (5 cm) in circular stockinette stitch before blocking.

FINISHED SIZE

About 8 inches (20.5 cm) around foot and 10¾ inches (27.5 cm) from top of leg to bottom of heel.

Note: You may want to wind your yarn into a center pull ball (by hand or on a ball winder) before beginning. This allows access to both ends of yarn and makes the Decorative Chain Stitch easier to work.

CLOCK PATTERN

(Worked over 3 stitches)

Rounds 1, 2, and 3: **P1, k1, p1.**

Rounds 4, 5, and 6: **K1, p1, k1.**

These 6 rounds make up the clock pattern.

LEG

Cast on 69 sts. Divide sts onto 4 needles placing 20 sts on needle #1, 15 sts on needles #2 and #3, and 19 sts on needle #4. Join into a round, being careful not to twist sts. This join is the "seam" line and marks the beginning of all future rounds. Purl 1 round. Knit 1 round, bringing working yarn to front when round is completed.

Add in a new strand of yarn (the other end of a center pull ball—see note at left) and work one round of Decorative Chain Stitch as follows:

Round 1: *K1 with new strand, p1 with original strand, leaving this strand forward; repeat from * ending k1.

Round 2: *P1 with original strand, leaving this strand forward, k1 with new strand; repeat from *, ending p1. Break off new strand.

Work k1, p1 ribbing for 7 rounds, dec 1 st on first round and inc 1 st on last round. Add in new strand of yarn and work 2 rounds of Decorative Chain Stitch as before. Break off new strand.

Knit 1 round, dec 1 st on needle #1. 68 sts remain.

Begin Clock Pattern and Shape Calf

Knit 19 sts on needle #1; begin working pattern as described at left and shown on chart and *at the same time* on the tenth round of the clock pattern begin shaping decreases on needles #1 and #4 as indicated on chart. Repeat this decrease round every 6 rounds 3 more times-4 times total. 60 sts remain.

Continue in established pattern until leg measures 8½ inches (21.5 cm) or desired length to top of heel. End having completed Round 6 of clock pattern ready to begin needle #4.

HEEL

Heel Flap

Begin with first st on needle #4. Knit 15 sts on needle #4 and 15 sts on needle #1 onto one needle, turn. P30, turn. These 30 sts form the heel flap. The remaining 30 sts will be held for the instep.

Row 1: *Sl 1, k1; repeat from *.

Row 2: Sl 1, p29.

Repeat the last 2 rows 14 more times for a total of 15 chain sts (see page 9) at each edge of heel flap.

Turn Heel

Row 1: Sl 1, k17, ssk, k1, turn.

Row 2: Sl 1, p5, p2tog, p1, turn.

Row 3: Sl 1, knit to within one st of the gap, ssk, k1, turn.

Row 4: Sl 1, purl to within one st of the gap, p2tog, p1, turn.

Repeat Rows 3 and 4 until all heel sts are worked. There are 18 heel sts.

Heel Gussets

Knit 18 heel sts, pick up and knit 15 chain sts along right side of heel flap. Work 30 instep sts, beginning with Round 1 of clock pattern. With an empty needle, pick up and knit 15 chain sts along left side of heel flap, knit 9 sts from heel needle. There are 24 sts on needles #1 and #4, 15 sts on needles #2 and #3.

Round 1: Work to 3 sts from end of needle #1, k2tog, k1. Work instep sts in established pattern. K1, ssk at beginning of needle #4, work to end.

Round 2: Work even in established pattern.

Repeat the last 2 rounds until there 15 sts on each needle. 60 sts total.

FOOT

Continue even in established pattern until foot measures 2½ inches (6.5 cm) less than desired finished length and you have completed Round 6 of clock pattern. Continue in stockinette stitch for ½ inch (1.3 cm).

Shape Toe

Round 1: *Work to last 2 sts on needle, k2tog; repeat from *.

Round 2: Work even.

Repeat the last 2 rounds until there are 8 sts on each needle. Work 1 round even. Work Round 1 (the decrease round) only until there are 8 sts remaining, 2 sts on each needle. Break yarn, thread tail through remaining sts, pull snug, and fasten off.

FINISHING

Weave in all ends. Block under a damp towel or on sock blockers.

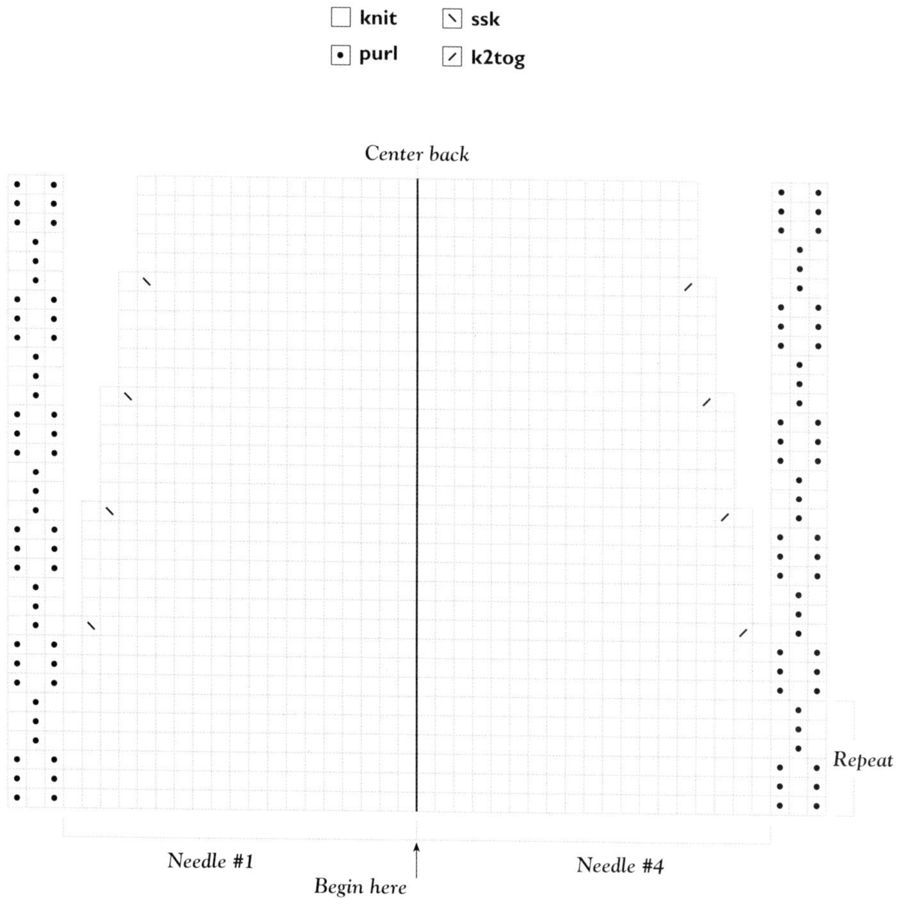

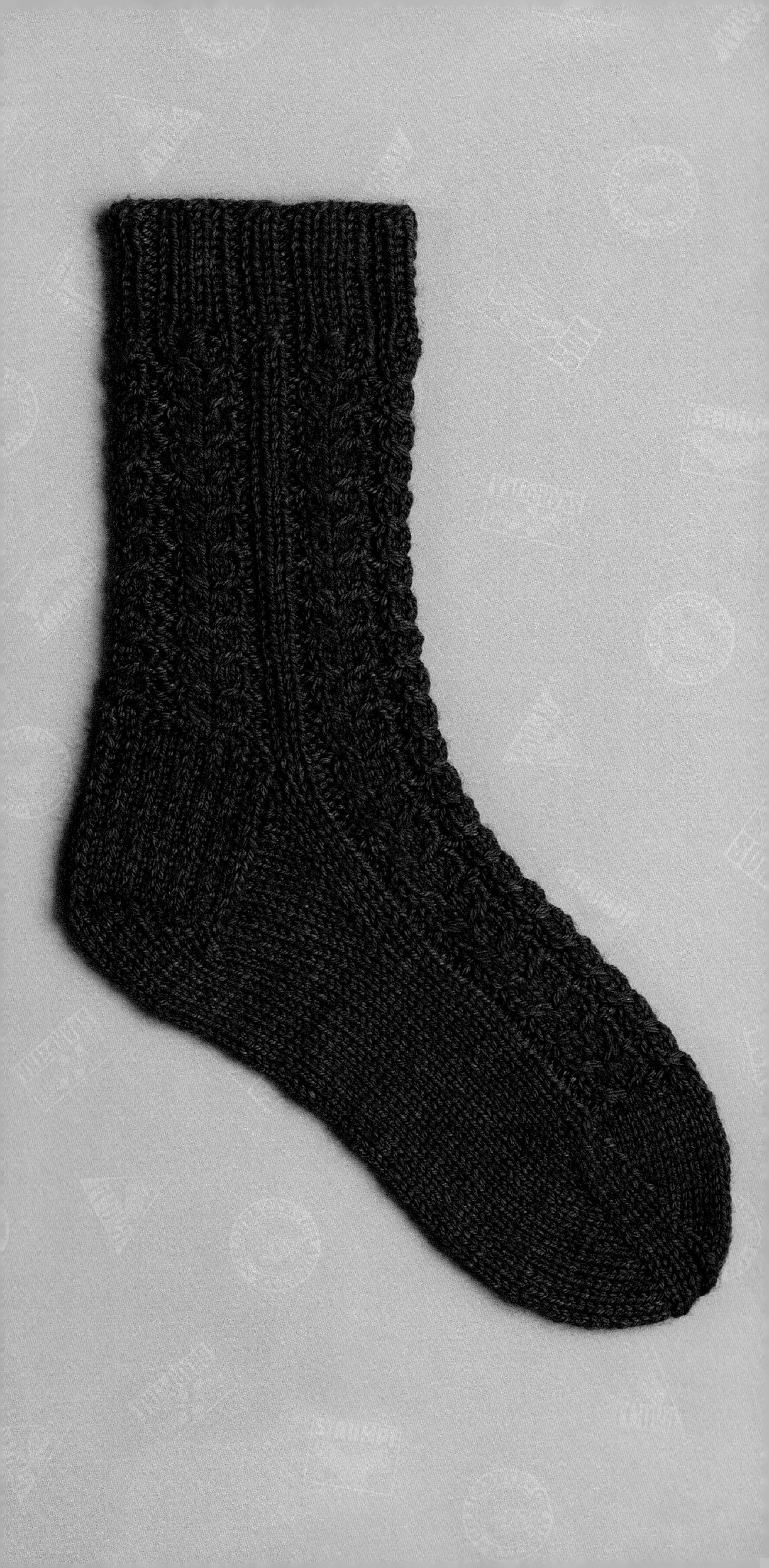

DENMARK

I have had the good fortune to travel with the Interweave Press Knitter's Journey to Scandinavia several times. We enjoy two weeks focused on knitting, but see many other sights as well! This sock is the product of an afternoon I spent in the National Museum in Copenhagen, studying the artifacts of early Danish history and Viking times. I marveled at the textiles, both the ancient and the reproductions, and was especially interested in rune stones and Viking art. The pattern on these socks comes from a design discovered on this day.

YARN

Happy Trails (90% wool, 10% nylon, 132 yd [120m]/50 g): Gunsmoke, 3 skeins.

NEEDLES

Set of five double-pointed needles size 3 (3.25 mm) or size needed to obtain correct gauge, cable needle.

GAUGE

12 sts and 14 rounds = 2 inches (5 cm) in circular stockinette stitch before blocking.

FINISHED SIZE

About 8½ inches (21.5 cm) around foot and 9 inches (23 cm) from top of leg to bottom of heel.

STITCHES

Left Cross **Slip 1 st onto cable needle and hold in front, k2, k1 from cable needle.**

Right Cross **Slip 2 sts onto cable needle and hold in back, k1, k2 from cable needle.**

LEG

Cast on 56 sts. Divide sts onto 4 needles, 16 sts on needles #1 and #3, 12 sts on needles #2 and #4. Join into a round, being careful not to twist sts. This join is the "seam" line and marks the beginning of all future rounds. The seam line is at the side of the sock—the center back is marked with a heavy line on the chart.

Rib: P1, *[k1, p1, k2, p1, k1, p2] 3 times, k2, p2; repeat from *, ending p1.

Work 11 rounds of rib pattern total.

Next Round: Work as established, adding a nupp stitch (see explanation on page 33) over each group of k2 sts.

Begin cable pattern as indicated on chart and work until leg measures 6½ inches (16.5 cm) or desired length to top of heel and you have completed one round after a cable turn.

HEEL

Heel Flap

Knit 26 sts onto needle #1, turn. P28, turn. These 28 sts form the heel flap. The remaining 28 sts will be held for the instep.

Row 1: *Sl 1, k1; repeat from *.

Row 2: Sl 1, p27.

Repeat the last 2 rows 13 more times for a total of 14 chain sts (see page 9) at each edge of heel flap.

Turn Heel

Row 1: Sl 1, k15, ssk, k1, turn.

Row 2: Sl 1, p5, p2tog, p1, turn.

Row 3: Sl 1, knit to within one st of the gap, ssk, k1, turn.

Row 4: Sl 1, purl to within one st of the gap, p2tog, p1, turn.

Repeat Rows 3 and 4 until all heel sts are worked, ending last repeat of Row 3 with the ssk, and last repeat of Row 4 with the p2tog. There are 16 heel sts.

Heel Gussets

Knit 16 heel sts, pick up and knit 14 chain sts along right side of heel flap. Work 28 instep sts in established pattern beginning with Round 2 onto needle #2. With an empty needle, pick up and knit 14 chain sts

Nupp Stitch

Bring right needle in front of next 2 sts. Insert it between the second st and the next st, under the left needle (figure 1). Wrap working yarn clockwise (opposite of usual wrap) around right needle and draw a loop through. Now wrap working yarn around right needle clockwise (figure 2), draw this wrap through the loop, and tighten yarn (figure 3). Place the right needle into the 2 wrapped sts on left needle as to purl and slip them onto the right needle (figure 4). Pass the new st over the top of these 2 sts and off the needle (figure 5).

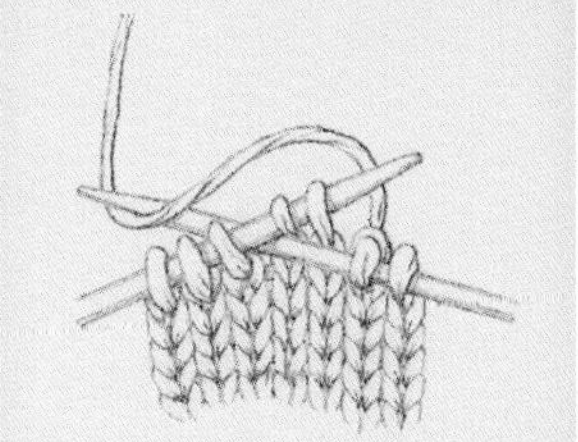

1

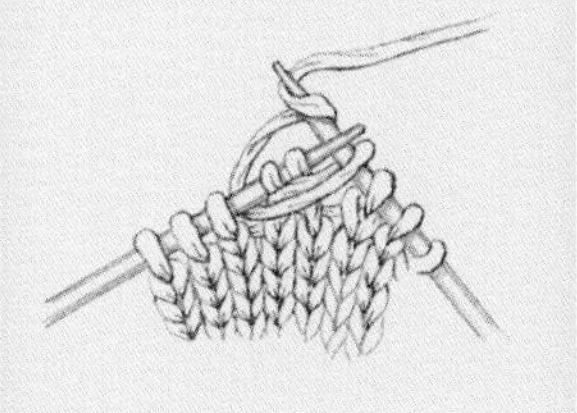

2

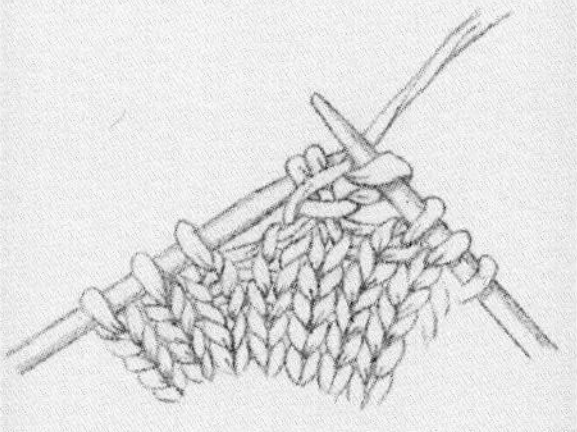

3

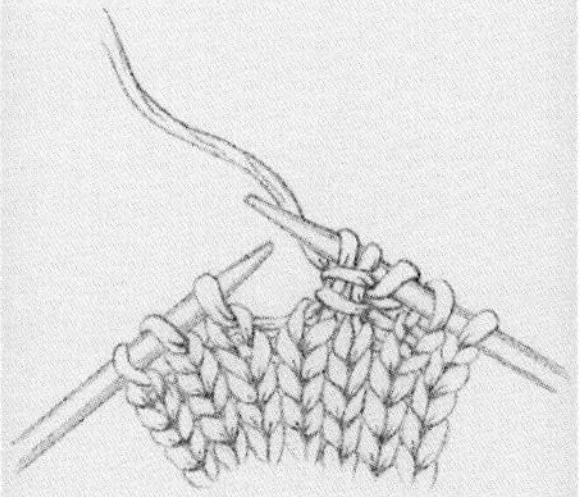

4

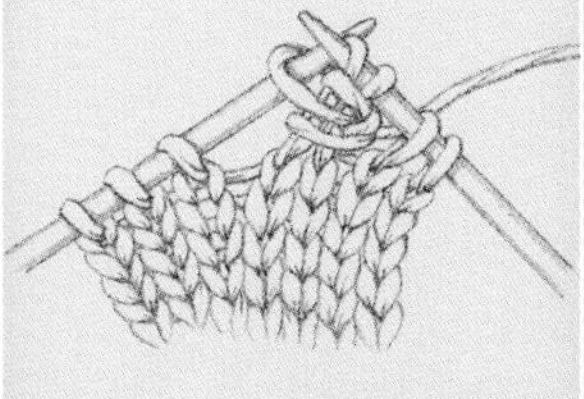

5

along left side of heel flap, knit 8 sts from heel needle. There are 22 sts on needles #1 and #3, 28 sts on needle #2.

Round 1: Work to 3 sts from end of needle #1, k2tog, k1. Work instep sts in established pattern. K1, ssk at beginning of needle #3, work to end.

Round 2: Work even in established pattern.

Repeat the last 2 rounds until there are 14 sts on needles #1 and #3. 56 sts total.

FOOT

Continue even in established pattern until foot measures 3 inches (7.5 cm) less than desired finished length and you have completed a cable round.

Shape Toe

Adjust sts onto 4 needles, 14 sts on each needle. Work 3 rounds in stockinette stitch.

Round 1: Work to 3 sts from end of needle #1, k2tog, k1. K1, ssk at beginning of needle #2, work to end of needle. Work to 3 sts from end of needle #3, k2tog, k1. K1, ssk at beginning of needle #4, work to end.

Round 2: Work even.

Repeat the last 2 rounds until there are 7 sts on each needle. Work Round 1 (the decrease round) only until there are 8 sts remaining, 2 sts on each needle. Break yarn, leaving a 12-inch (30.5-cm) tail. Place the sts from needles #1 and #4 onto one needle and the other 4 sts onto another needle. Kitchener stitch these sts together (see page 9).

FINISHING

Weave in all ends. Block under a damp towel or on sock blockers.

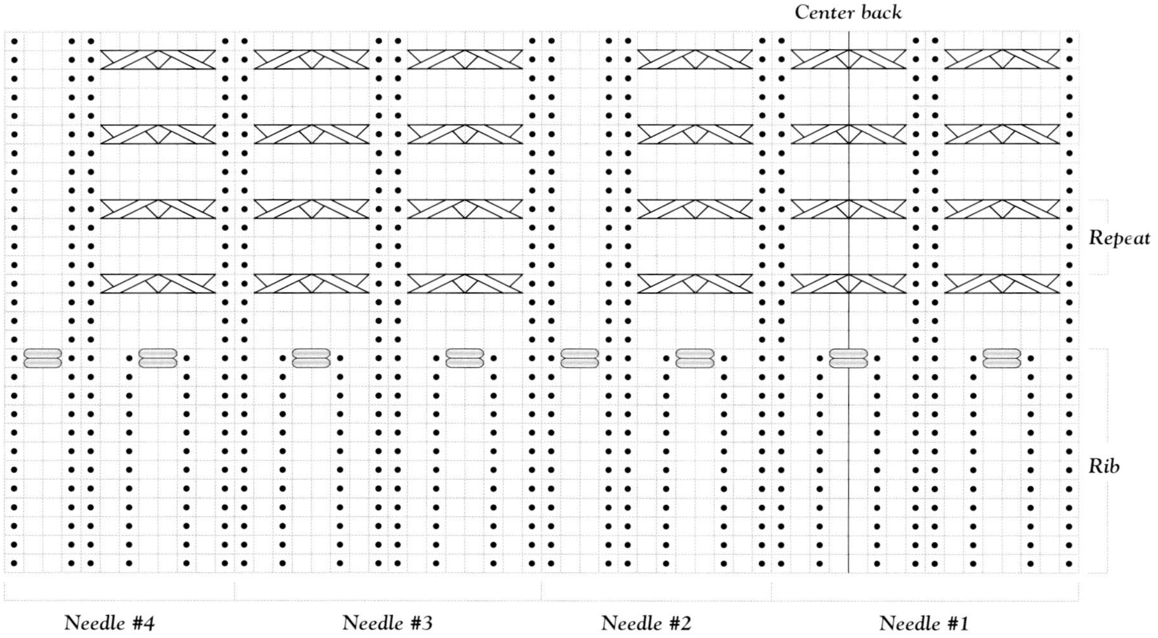

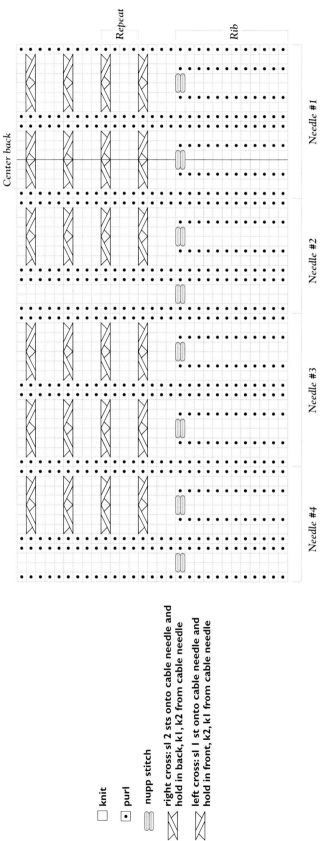

- knit
- purl
- nupp stitch
- right cross: sl 2 sts onto cable needle and hold in back, k1, k2 from cable needle
- left cross: sl 1 st onto cable needle and hold in front, k2, k1 from cable needle

FRIDAY HARBOR

One of my favorite places in the United States is the Pacific Northwest. I love the forests, the tulip fields, the beaches, and the views of the ocean. These socks are reminiscent of my many wonderful visits to Coupeville on Whidbey Island, Anacortes, and the San Juan Islands. Whether vacationing or teaching, it has always been a delight to visit this part of the country. The color was chosen because of the lush forests, and the pattern reminds me of the wake a sailboat leaves as it glides by on a misty morning.

YARN

Mountain Colors Weaver's Wool Quarters (100% wool, 350 yd [320 m]/100 g): Evergreen, 1 skein.

NEEDLES

Set of five double-pointed needles size 2 (2.75 mm) or size needed to obtain correct gauge.

GAUGE

12 sts and 18 rounds = 2 inches (5 cm) in circular stockinette stitch before blocking.

FINISHED SIZE

About 7¾ inches (19.5 cm) around foot and 9½ inches (24 cm) from top of leg to bottom of heel.

LEG

Cast on 50 sts. Divide sts onto 3 needles (13 sts on needle #1, 25 sts on needle #2, 12 sts on needle #3). Join into a round, being careful not to twist sts. This join is the "seam" line and marks the beginning of all future rounds. Purl 1 round. Knit 1 round. Work cuff chart as indicated, and *at the same time* k2tog on needle #1 on last round of cuff. 49 sts remain.

Continue following chart and work until leg measures 8 inches (20.5 cm) or desired length to top of heel. End having worked Round 19 of chart over instep sts and ready to begin needle #3—last 12 sts of round.

HEEL

Heel Flap

Begin with first st on needle #3. Work sl 1, k1 over 12 sts on needle #3 and 12 sts on needle #1 onto one needle, turn. P24, turn. These 24 sts form the heel flap. The remaining 25 sts will be held for the instep.

Row 1: *Sl 1, k1; repeat from *, turn.

Row 2: Sl 1, p23.

Repeat the last 2 rows 11 more times for a total of 12 chain sts (see page 9) at each edge of heel flap.

Turn Heel

Row 1: Sl 1, k13, ssk, k1, turn.

Row 2: Sl 1, p5, p2tog, p1, turn.

Row 3: Sl 1, knit to within one st of the gap, ssk, k1, turn.

Row 4: Sl 1, purl to within one st of the gap, p2tog, p1, turn.

Repeat Rows 3 and 4 until all heel sts are worked, ending last repeat of Row 3 with ssk, and last repeat of Row 4 with p2tog. There are 14 heel sts.

Heel Gussets
Knit 14 heel sts, pick up and knit 12 chain sts along right side of heel flap. Work 25 instep sts in established pattern (this will be Round 20, a knit round). ***Note:*** From now on the 2 purl sts at each edge of the pattern will be knit, not purled. With an empty needle, pick up and knit 12 chain sts along left side of heel flap, knit 7 sts from heel needle. There are 19 sts on needles #1 and #3, 25 sts on needle #2.

Round 1: Work to 3 sts from end of needle #1, k2tog, k1. Work instep sts in established pattern. K1, ssk at beginning of needle #3, work to end.

Round 2: Work even in established pattern.

Repeat the last 2 rounds until there are 12 sts on needles #1 and #3. 49 sts total.

FOOT

Continue even in established pattern until there are 7 repeats total of the 20-row lace pattern. Continue according to chart, making 2 more small diamond patterns. Decrease 1 st on needle #2 on last round. 48 sts remain.

Continue in stockinette stitch until foot measures 2½ inches (6.5 mm) less than desired finished length. Adjust sts so there are 16 sts on each needle.

Shape Toe

First Decrease Round: *K6, k2tog; repeat from *.

Work 6 rounds even.

Second Decrease Round: *K5, k2tog; repeat from *.

Work 5 rounds even.

Third Decrease Round: *K4, k2tog; repeat from *.

Work 4 rounds even.

Fourth Decrease Round: *K3, k2tog; repeat from *.

Work 3 rounds even.

Fifth Decrease Round: *K2, k2tog; repeat from *.

Work 2 rounds even.

Sixth Decrease Round: *K1, k2tog; repeat from *.

Work 1 round even.

Seventh Decrease Round: *K2tog; repeat from *.

There are 6 sts remaining. Break yarn, thread tail through remaining sts, pull snug, and fasten off.

FINISHING

Weave in all ends. Block under a damp towel or on sock blockers.

Friday Harbor - chart 2

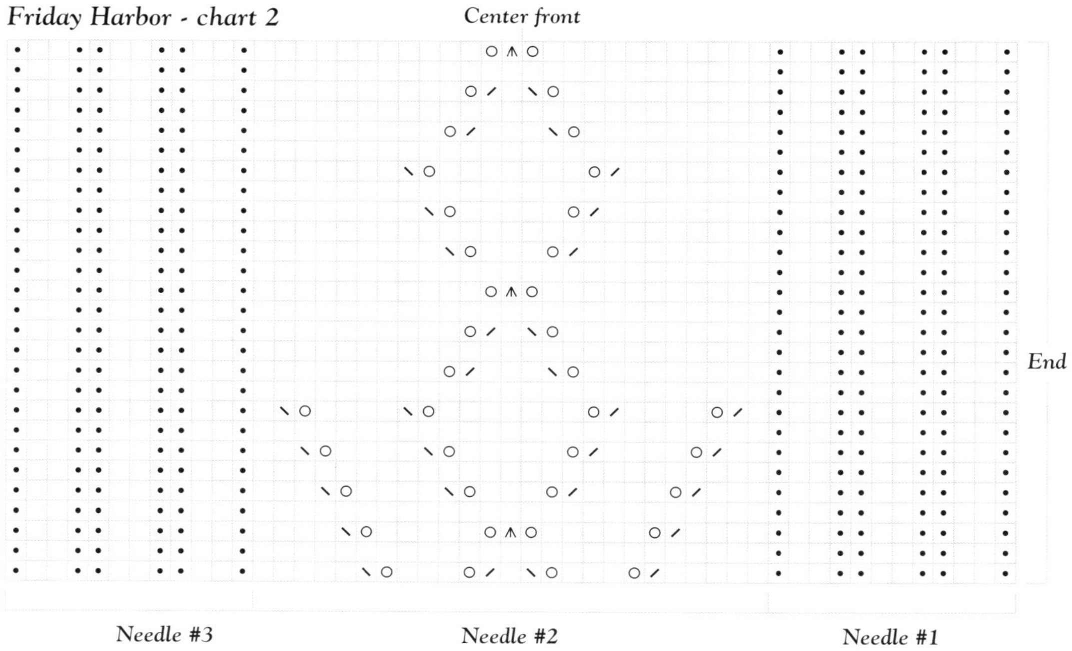

- knit
- purl
- yarn over
- sl 2tog knitwise, k1, p2sso
- ssk
- k2tog

Friday Harbor - chart 1

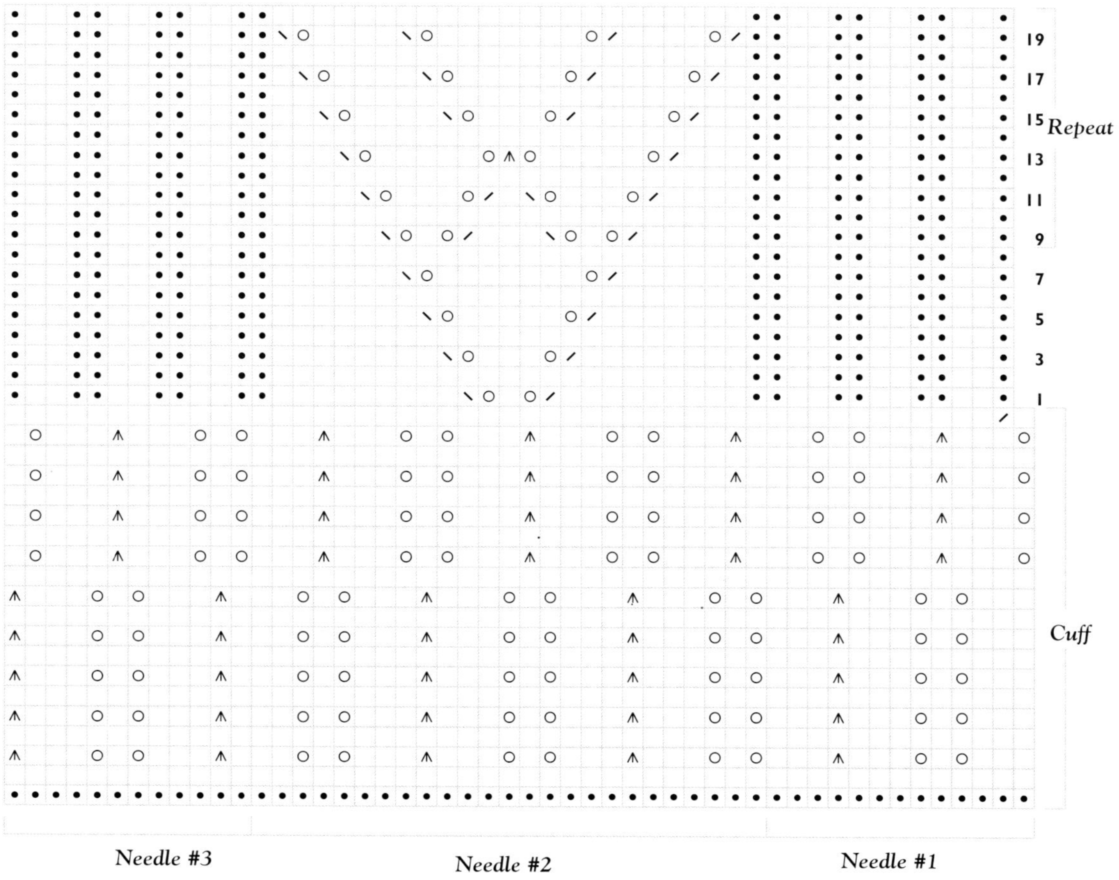

STRUMPF
STRUMPF

HIIUMAA MISMATCHED MATES

This sock, coupled with the one shown on page 46, comes from a "pair" of socks I purchased at a small mill shop on the Estonian island of Hiiumaa. Shopping for a gift for my sweetheart, I poked through a basketful of hand knitted socks, looking for just the right pair. I narrowed my selection down to what I thought was a nice pair. Looking closer, I realized they were both striped, but not with the same pattern. I liked both patterns and thought, why not—at least the colors match! Every time I see the originals, I smile at the memory of their purchase. You can make two mismatched mates, or two pairs with matching mates.

HIIUMAA MATES # 1

YARN

Brown Sheep Company Naturespun 3 Ply Sport (100% wool, 184 yd [168 m]/50 g): #701 Stone (MC), 2 skeins, #720 Ash (CC), 1 skein. This amount makes a matched or mismatched pair of either design.

NEEDLES

Set of five double-pointed needles size 1 (2.25 mm) or size needed to obtain correct gauge.

GAUGE

15 sts and 22 rounds = 2 inches (5 cm) in circular stockinette stitch before blocking.

FINISHED SIZE

About 9 inches (23 cm) around foot and 9½ inches (24 cm) from top of leg to bottom of heel.

LEG

With CC, cast on 72 sts. Divide sts evenly onto 4 needles (18 sts on each needle) and join into a round, being careful not to twist sts. This join is the "seam" line and marks the beginning of all future rounds. Work k1, p1 ribbing for 2 rounds. Join MC and continue in ribbing, working colors as follows: 5 rounds MC, (2 rounds CC, 2 rounds MC) twice, 2 rounds CC, 5 rounds MC, 2 rounds CC, 2 rounds MC, 2 rounds CC, 5 rounds MC, 2 rounds CC.

Begin stockinette stitch and work striped pattern as follows:

*5 rounds MC, [2 rounds CC, 2 rounds MC] twice, 2 rounds CC, 5 rounds MC, 2 rounds CC, 2 rounds MC, 2 rounds CC, 5 rounds MC, 2 rounds CC. Repeat from * for the leg and foot and *at the same time* when work measures 7 inches (18 cm) and the second group of 3 CC stripes has been completed, begin heel.

HEEL

Heel Flap

With MC, knit 18 sts on needle #1, turn. P36, turn. These 36 sts form the heel flap. The remaining 36 sts will be held for the instep.

Row 1: *Sl 1, k1; repeat from *.

Row 2: Sl 1, p35.

Row 3: Sl 1 *sl 1, k1; repeat from * ending last repeat k2.

Row 4: Sl 1, p35.

Repeat the last 4 rows 8 more times for a total of 18 chain sts (see page 9) at each edge of heel flap.

Turn Heel

Row 1: Work 23 sts in established pattern, ssk, turn.

Row 2: Sl 1, p10, p2tog, turn.

Row 3: Sl 1, work 10 sts in established pattern, ssk, turn.

Row 4: Sl 1, p10, p2tog, turn.

Repeat Rows 3 and 4 until all heel sts are worked. There are 12 heel sts.

Heel Gussets

With MC, knit 12 heel sts, pick up and knit 18 chain sts along right side of heel flap. Work 36 instep sts. With an empty needle, pick up and knit 18 chain sts along left side of heel flap, knit 6 sts from heel needle. There are 24 sts on needles #1 and #4, 18 sts on needles #2 and #3.

Round 1: Work to 3 sts from end of needle #1, k2tog, k1. Work instep sts in established pattern. K1, ssk at beginning of needle #4, work to end.

Round 2: Work even in established pattern.

Repeat the last 2 rounds until there are 18 sts on needles #1 and #4. 72 sts total.

FOOT

Continue even in established striped pattern until three complete patterns have been worked. Change pattern to 5 rounds MC and 2 rounds CC until foot measures 2 inches (5 cm) less than desired finished length.

Shape Toe

Keeping established striped pattern, work as follows:

First decrease round: *K6, k2tog; repeat from *.

Work 6 rounds even.

Second decrease round: *K5, k2tog; repeat from *.

Work 5 rounds even.

Third decrease round: *K4, k2tog; repeat from *.

Work 4 rounds even.

Fourth decrease round: *K3, k2tog; repeat from *.

Work 3 rounds even.

Fifth decrease round: *K2, k2tog; repeat from *.

Work 2 rounds even.

Sixth decrease round: *K1, k2tog; repeat from *.

Work 1 round even.

Seventh decrease round: *K2tog; repeat from *. 9 sts remain.

Break yarn, thread tail through remaining sts, pull snug, and fasten off.

FINISHING

Weave in all ends. Block under a damp towel or on sock blockers.

HIIUMAA MATES # 2

YARN

Brown Sheep Company Naturespun 3 Ply Sport (100% wool, 184 yd [168 m]/50 g): #701 Stone (MC), 2 skeins; #720 Ash (CC), 1 skein. This amount makes a matched or mismatched pair of either design.

NEEDLES

Set of five double-pointed needles size 1 (2.25 mm) or size needed to obtain correct gauge.

GAUGE

15 sts and 22 rounds = 2 inches (5 cm) in circular stockinette stitch before blocking.

FINISHED SIZE

About 9 inches (23 cm) around foot and 9½ inches (24 cm) from top of leg to bottom of heel.

STRUMPF
SOK

LEG

With MC, cast on 72 sts. Divide sts evenly onto 4 needles (18 sts on each needle) and join into a round, being careful not to twist sts. This join is the "seam" line and marks the beginning of all future rounds. Work k1, p1 ribbing for 7 rounds. Join CC and continue in ribbing, working colors as follows: 3 rounds CC, [1 round MC, 1 round CC] twice, 1 round MC, 3 rounds CC, 7 rounds MC, [1 round CC, 1 round MC] twice, 1 round CC, 3 rounds MC.

Begin stockinette stitch and work striped pattern as follows: 9 rounds MC, 1 round CC, 1 round MC, 1 round CC, 21 rounds MC, 1 round CC, 1 round MC, 1 round CC, and *at the same time* when work measures 7 inches (18 cm) and 14 rounds MC have been completed, begin heel.

HEEL

Heel Flap

With MC, knit 18 sts on needle #1, turn. P36, turn. These 36 sts form the heel flap. The remaining 36 sts will be held for the instep.

Row 1: *Sl 1, k1, repeat from *.

Row 2: Sl 1, p35.

Row 3: Sl 1 *sl 1, k1, repeat from * ending last repeat k2.

Row 4: Sl 1, p35.

Repeat the last 4 rows 8 more times for a total of 18 chain sts (see page 9) at each edge of heel flap.

Turn Heel

Row 1: Work 23 sts in established pattern, ssk, turn.

Row 2: Sl 1, p10, p2tog, turn.

Row 3: Sl 1, work 10 sts in established pattern, ssk, turn.

Row 4: Sl 1, p10, p2tog.

Repeat Rows 3 and 4 until all heel sts are worked. There are 12 heel sts.

Heel Gussets

With MC, knit 12 heel sts, pick up and knit 18 chain sts along right side of heel flap. Work 36 instep sts. With an empty needle, pick up and knit 18 chain sts along left side of heel flap, knit 6 sts from heel needle. There are 24 sts on needles #1 and #4, 18 sts on needles #2 and #3.

Round 1: Work to 3 sts from the end of needle #1, k2tog, k1. Work instep sts as established. K1, ssk at beginning of needle #4, work to end.

Round 2: Work even in established pattern.

Repeat the last 2 rounds until there are 18 sts on needles #1 and #4. 72 sts total.

FOOT

Continue even with MC until there are 28 rounds of MC from last CC stripe. Work 1 round CC, 1 round MC, 1 round CC, 35 rounds MC, 1 round CC, 1 round MC, 1 round CC. Cut CC. With MC, work until foot measures 2 inches (5 cm) less than desired finished length, working at least 1 round of MC before beginning toe shaping.

Shape Toe

First decrease round: *K6, k2tog; repeat from *.

Work 6 rounds even.

Second decrease round: *K5, k2tog; repeat from *.

Work 5 rounds even.

Third decrease round: *K4, k2tog; repeat from *.

Work 4 rounds even.

Fourth decrease round: *K3, k2tog; repeat from *.

Work 3 rounds even.

Fifth decrease round: *K2, k2tog; repeat from *.

Work 2 rounds even.

Sixth decrease round: *K1, k2tog; repeat from *.

Work 1 round even.

Seventh decrease round: *K2tog; repeat from *. 9 sts remain.

Break yarn, thread tail through remaining sts, pull snug, and fasten off.

FINISHING

Weave in all ends. Block under a damp towel or on sock blockers.

HURON MOUNTAIN

These striped socks were born during an extraordinary vacation to the Upper Peninsula of Michigan. We stayed at a community of log cabins, complete with a clubhouse, along the shores of Lake Superior. Our days were spent playing on the beach and canoeing and rowing on pristine lakes. It was here that I saw and heard my very first loon. What a beautifully decorated and graceful bird. I love multiple patterns and the loon had it all. I was so impressed with the show put on by the feathered creature that I spent my nights designing some socks to commemorate the event.

YARN

Brown Sheep Company Wildfoote (75% wool, 25% nylon, 215 yd [197 m]/50 g): SY05 Black Orchid (MC), 2 skeins; SY10 Vanilla (CC), 1 skein.

NEEDLES

Set of five double pointed needles size 1 (2.25 mm) or size needed to obtain correct gauge.

GAUGE

16 sts and 18 rounds = 2 inches (5 cm) in circular stockinette st before blocking.

FINISHED SIZE

About 8 inches (20.5 cm) around foot and 9 inches (23 cm) from top of leg to bottom of heel.

LEG

With MC, cast on 72 sts. Divide sts evenly onto 4 needles (18 sts on each needle) and join into a round, being careful not to twist sts. This join is the "seam" line and marks the beginning of all future rounds. Work k2, p1 ribbing for 2 inches (5 cm). Change to stockinette stitch and follow charts 1 and 2. When leg measures 7½ inches (19 cm) or desired length to heel and you have worked the first MC round after the third "lice" round, begin heel flap. (Lice is a term used to describe a dot pattern in knitting.)

HEEL

Heel Flap

Knit 18 sts on needle #1, turn. P36, turn. These 36 sts form the heel flap. The remaining 36 sts will be held for the instep.

Row 1: *Sl 1, k35.

Row 2: Sl 1, p35.

Repeat the last 2 rows 8 more times for a total of 9 chain sts (see page 9) at each edge of heel flap.

Shape Heel

Row 1: Sl 1, k11, k2tog, k8, ssk, k12, turn.

Row 2: Sl 1, p33, turn.

Row 3: Sl 1, k10, k2tog, k8, ssk, k11, turn.

Row 4: Sl 1, p31, turn.

Row 5: Sl 1, k9, k2tog, k8, ssk, k10, turn.

Row 6: Sl 1, p29, turn.

Row 7: Sl 1, k8, k2tog, k8, ssk, k9, turn.

Row 8: Sl 1, p27, turn.

There are 28 sts for turning the heel.

Turn Heel

Row 1: Sl 1, k17, ssk, turn.

Row 2: Sl 1, p8, p2tog, turn.

Row 3: Sl 1, k8, ssk, turn.

Row 4: Sl 1, p8, p2tog, turn.

Repeat Rows 3 and 4 until all heel sts are worked. There are 10 heel sts.

Heel Gussets

With MC, knit 10 heel sts, pick up and knit 13 chain sts along right side of heel flap. Work 36 instep sts in established pattern. With an empty needle, pick up and knit 13 chain sts along left side of heel flap, knit 5 sts from heel needle. There are 18 sts on each needle. 72 sts total.

FOOT

Continue with chart 3 until foot measures 2 inches (5 cm) less than desired finished length.

Shape Toe

Round 1: *Work to last 2 sts on needle, k2tog; repeat from *.

Round 2: Work even.

Repeat the last 2 rounds until there are 9 sts on each needle. Work Round 1 (the decrease round) only until there are 8 sts remaining, 2 sts on each needle. Break yarn, thread tail through remaining sts, pull snug, and fasten off.

FINISHING

Weave in all ends. Block under a damp towel or on sock blockers.

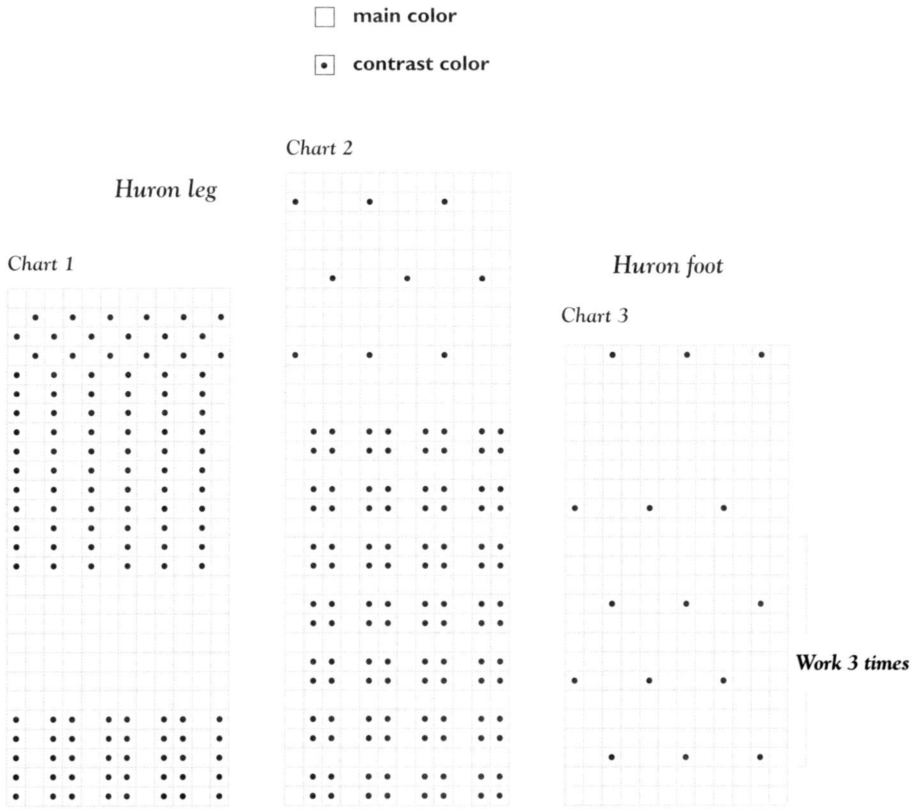

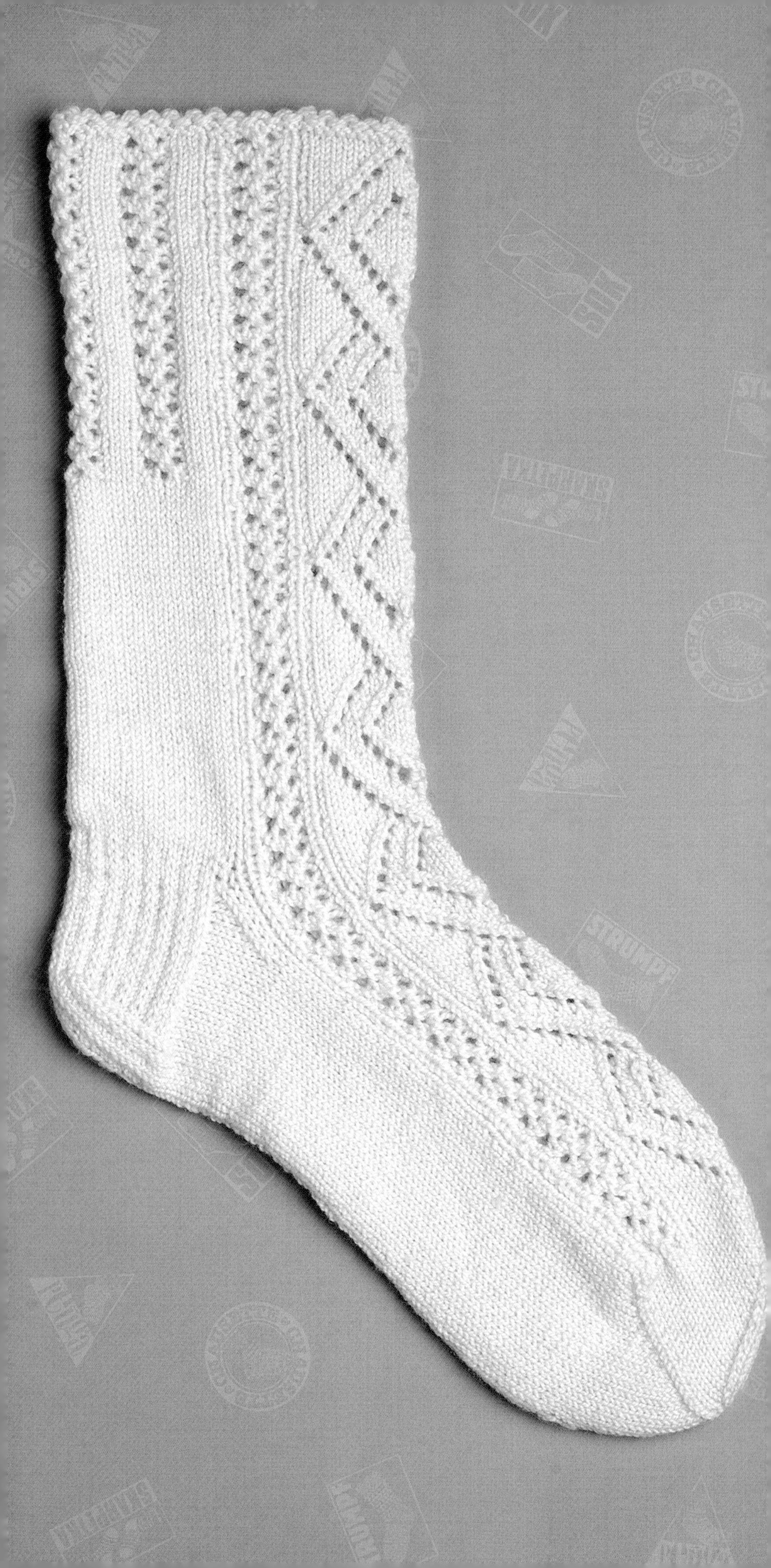

NEW ENGLAND

These elegant socks were created to honor many special visits to New England—all in the line of duty, teaching workshops to knitters! I have seen many lovely old stockings there, from the Shaker knitting at Enfield Village in New Hampshire to a collection of city finery brought to a workshop by a student. I imagine these socks to be something like the fancy stockings a lady would have worn to a contra dance in the village hall. You may have to watch the chart while knitting these socks, especially while working the center diamond, but the results are worth the effort!

YARN

Koigu Merino (100% Merino wool, 175 yd [160 m]/50 g): Natural, 3 skeins.

NEEDLES

Set of five double-pointed needles size 0 (2 mm) or size needed to obtain correct gauge.

GAUGE

18 sts and 24 rounds = 2 inches (5 cm) in circular stockinette stitch before blocking.

FINISHED SIZE

About 7¾ inches (19.5 cm) around foot and 9½ inches (24 cm) from top of leg to bottom of heel.

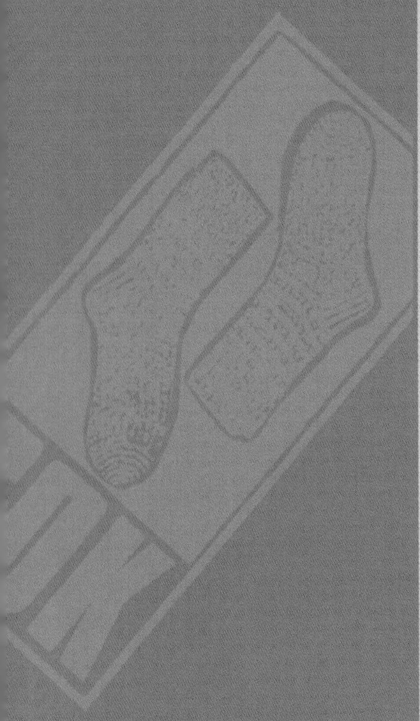

LEG

Cast on 70 sts using a Double Start Cast-on with the strand over the thumb doubled (see page 7). Divide sts onto 3 needles (19 sts on needle #1, 35 sts on needle #2, 16 sts on needle #3). Join into a round, being careful not to twist sts. This join is the "seam" line and marks the beginning of all future rounds. Knit 1 round. Purl 1 round.

Begin chart as indicated. Work until leg measures 4 inches (10 cm), discontinue back lacy ribbing, and continue in stockinette stitch. Dec 1 st on next round by knitting together the last 2 sts on needle #1. 69 sts remain. Continue in established pattern until leg measures 8 inches (20.5 cm) or desired length to top of heel. End having completed four Diamond patterns, ending on Round 12.

HEEL

Heel Flap

Knit 18 sts on needle #1, turn. P34, turn. These 34 sts form the heel flap. The remaining 35 sts will be held for the instep.

Row 1: *Sl 1, k1; repeat from *.

Row 2: Sl 1, p33.

Repeat the last 2 rows 16 more times for a total of 17 chain sts (see page 9) at each edge of heel flap.

Turn Heel

Row 1: Sl 1, k1 over 21 sts, ssk, turn.

Row 2: Sl 1, p8, p2tog, turn.

Row 3: (Sl 1, k1) 4 times, s1 1, ssk, turn.

Row 4: Sl 1, p8, p2tog, turn.

Repeat Rows 3 and 4 until all heel sts are worked. There are 10 heel sts.

Heel Gussets

Knit 10 heel sts, pick up and knit 17 chain sts along right side of heel flap. Work 35 instep sts in established pattern beginning with Round 1. With an empty needle, pick up and knit 17 chain sts along left side of heel flap, knit 5 sts from heel needle. There are 22 sts on needles #1 and #3, 35 sts on needle #2.

Round 1: Work to 3 sts from end of needle #1, k2tog, k1. Work instep sts in established pattern. K1, ssk at beginning of needle #3, work to end.

Round 2: Work even in established pattern.

Repeat the last 2 rounds until there are 17 sts on needles #1 and #3. 69 sts total.

FOOT

Continue even in established pattern until there are 7 completed repeats of Diamond pattern and foot measures 2 inches (5 cm) less than desired finished length.

Next Round: Work in stockinette stitch, decreasing 1 st. 68 sts remain.

Shape Toe

Adjust sts onto 4 needles, 17 sts on each needle.

Round 1: *Knit to 2 sts from end of needle, k2tog; repeat from * to end of round.

Round 2: Work even in stockinette stitch.

Repeat the last 2 rounds until there are 9 sts on each needle. Work Round 1 (the decrease round) only until there are 8 sts remaining, 2 sts on each needle. Break yarn, thread tail through remaining sts, pull snug, and fasten off.

FINISHING

Weave in all ends. Block under a damp towel or on sock blockers.

New England - chart 2

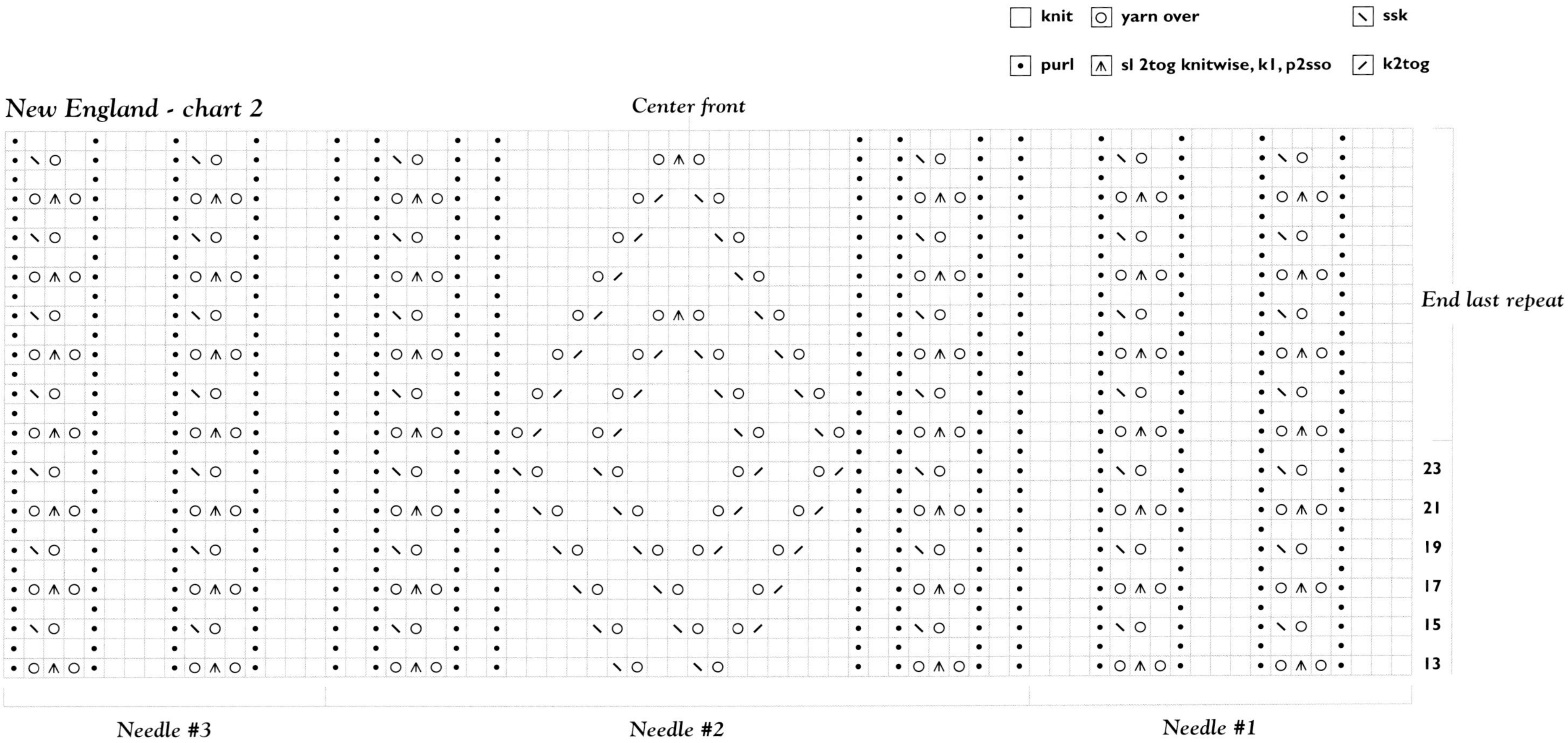

New England - chart 1

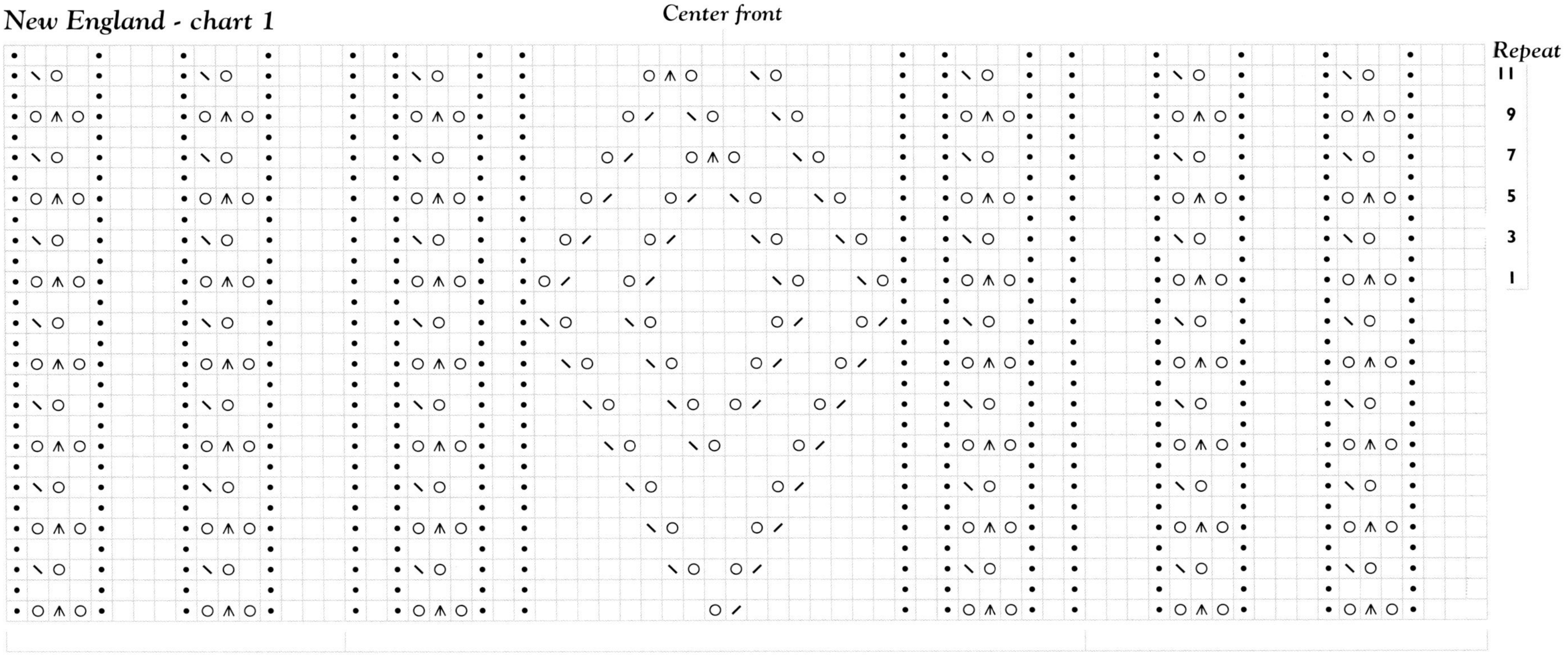

SOK
STRUMPF

THE ROAD TO OSLO

My good friend Annemor Sundbø suggested these quick-to-knit socks. In her wonderful book, *Everyday Knitting, Treasures from a ragpile* (English translation, Torridal Tweed: kristiansand, 2000), she talks about the wealth of knitting she discovered in her factory for recycled wool. These socks were designed from a pair in her collection. She told me, "It was a fashion for both men and women to wear these socks from the early 1920s for skiing. The cuff was folded over the ski boots, to prevent the snow coming into the boots. I can remember socks like this in my grandmother's home. When these socks came with patterns and knitting instructions in women's magazines, it was a fashion all over Norway."

YARN

Aurora Yarns Viking Raggsokkengarn (80% Norwegian wool, 20% nylon 109 yd [100 m]/50 g): #2 Light Gray (MC), 2 skeins; #11 Red (CC1) and #3 Gray Mix (CC2), 1 skein each.

NEEDLES

Set of five double-pointed needles size 4 (3.5 mm) and size 3 (3.25 mm) or size needed to obtain correct gauge.

GAUGE

12 sts and 14 rounds = 2 inches (5 cm) in circular stockinette stitch before blocking.

FINISHED SIZE

About 8½ inches (21.5 cm) around foot and 5¼ inches (13.5 cm) from top of leg to bottom of heel (with cuff turned down).

Note: The hem at the cuff may be worked several ways. An eyelet edge is outlined below. You may use a provisional cast-on and sew the resulting live stitches down, or cast on with waste yarn, removing the waste yarn after the sock is completed and sewing the resulting live stitches down.

LEG

With CC2 and smaller needles, cast on 54 sts. Divide sts onto 4 needles (13 sts on needles #1 and #3, 14 sts on needles #2 and #4). Join into a round, being careful not to twist sts. This join is the "seam" line and marks the beginning of all future rounds. Work 2 rounds stockinette stitch.

Next Round: *YO, k2tog; repeat from *.

Change to larger needles and work 3 rounds stockinette stitch. Work chart as indicated. When chart in complete, work 1 round stockinette stitch. Change to smaller needles and work 6 rounds stockinette stitch.

Next Round: *K7, k2tog; repeat from *. 48 sts remain.

Work 7 more rounds stockinette stitch—15 stockinette stitch rounds total. Break off CC2. Attach MC and turn work inside out (so the cuff will fold to the outside) and continue in stockinette stitch for 8 rounds or desired length to top of heel.

HEEL

Heel Flap

Knit 12 sts, turn. P24, turn. These 24 sts form the heel flap. The remaining 24 sts will be held for the instep.

Row 1: Sl 1, k23.

Row 2: Sl 1, p23.

Repeat the last 2 rows 11 more times for a total of 12 chain sts (see page 9) at each edge of heel flap.

Turn Heel

Row 1: K14, ssk, k1, turn.

Row 2: Sl 1, p5, p2tog, p1, turn.

Row 3: Sl 1, knit to within 1 st of the gap, ssk, k1, turn.

Row 4: Sl 1, purl to within 1 st of the gap, p2tog, p1, turn.

Repeat Rows 3 and 4 until all heel sts are worked, ending last repeat of Row 3 with the ssk and last repeat of Row 4 with the p2tog. There are 14 heel sts.

Heel Gussets

Knit 14 heel sts, pick up and knit 12 chain sts along right side of heel flap. Work 24 instep sts. With an empty needle, pick up and knit 12 chain sts along left side of heel flap, knit 7 sts from heel needle. There are 19 sts on needles #1 and #4, 12 sts on needles #2 and #3.

Round 1: Work to 3 sts from end of needle #1, k2tog, k1. Work instep sts. K1, ssk at beginning of needle #4, work to end.

Round 2: Work even in established pattern.

Repeat the last 2 rounds until there are 12 sts on needles #1 and #4. 48 sts total.

FOOT

Continue even until foot measures 2½ inches (6.5 cm) less than desired finished length.

Shape Toe

Round 1: Work to 3 sts from end of needle #1, k2tog, k1. K1, ssk at beginning of needle #2. Work to 3 sts from end of needle #3, k2tog, k1. K1, ssk at beginning of needle #4, work to end.

Round 2: Work even.

Repeat the last 2 rounds until there are 6 sts on each needle. Work Round 1 (the decrease round) only until there are 8 sts remaining, 2 sts on each needle. Place the stitches on needles #1 and #4 onto one needle and the stitches on needles #2 and #3 onto another needle. Kitchener stitch (see page 9) these 2 sets of 4 stitches together.

FINISHING

Fold hem to inside along eyelet round and sew down. Weave in all ends. Block under a damp towel or on sock blockers.

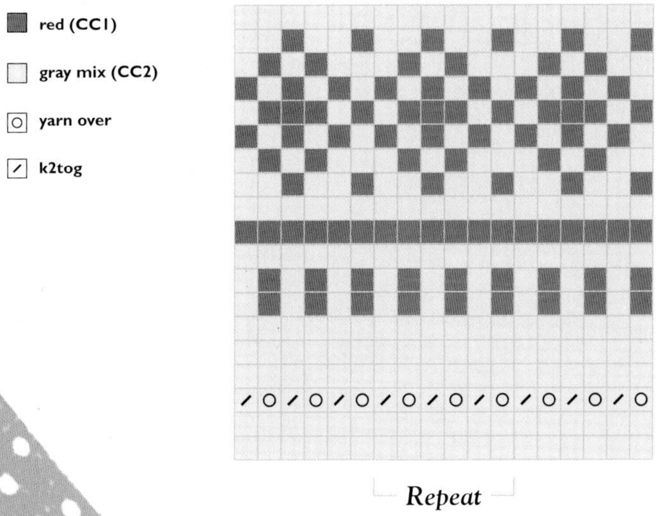

STRUMPF

SANTA FE

I spent many summers during my childhood in New Mexico. We always made at least one visit to Santa Fe, where we enjoyed a long-awaited lunch at The Shed and wandered through the shops as though they were galleries. There was always so much to see. Now grown up, I still enjoy visiting this colorful, exotic place, though it has changed a lot in the passing years. The design for this sock was taken from a Navajo rug pattern and the colors reflect the sand, the jewelry, and the blooming Chamisa found in this Southwestern paradise.

YARN

Happy Trails Sock Yarn (90% wool, 10% nylon, 132 yd [120 m]/50 g): Buckskin (MC), 2 skeins; Rabbit Brush (CC1) and Turquoise (CC2), 1 skein each.

NEEDLES

Set of five doubled-pointed needles size 3 (3.25 mm) or size needed to obtain correct gauge.

GAUGE

12 sts and 14 rounds = 2 inches (5 cm) in circular stockinette stitch before blocking.

FINISHED SIZE

About 8½ (9¼) inches (21.5 [23.5] cm) around foot and 9 (9½) inches (23 [24] cm) from top of leg to bottom of heel.

LEG

With MC, cast on 50 (55) sts using a Double Start Cast-on with the strand over the thumb doubled (see page 7). Divide sts onto 4 needles—12 (14) sts on needles #1 and #2, 13 (14) sts on needle #3, and 13 sts on needle #4. Join into a round, being careful not to twist sts. This join is the "seam" line and marks the beginning of all future rounds. Knit 1 round. Purl 1 round. Knit 2 rounds. Purl 1 round.

Change to stockinette stitch and follow chart as indicated. When leg chart is complete, cut CC1 and CC2. Continue in stockinette stitch with MC until leg measures 7 (8) inches (18 [20.5] cm) or desired length to top of heel.

HEEL

Heel Flap

Knit 12 (14) sts on needle #1, turn. P25 (27), turn. These 25 (27) sts form the heel flap. The remaining 25 (28) sts will be held for the instep.

Row 1: *Sl 1, k1; repeat from * ending last repeat k2.

Row 2: Sl 1, p24 (26).

Repeat the last 2 rows 12 (13) more times for a total of 13 (14) chain sts (see page 9) at each edge of heel flap.

Turn Heel

Row 1: (Sl 1, k1) over 16 (18) sts, sl 1, k1, psso, turn.

Row 2: Sl 1, p7 (9), p2tog, turn.

Row 3: (Sl 1, k1) over 8 (10) sts, sl 1, k1, psso, turn.

Row 4: Sl 1, p7 (9), p2tog, turn.

Repeat Rows 3 and 4 until all heel sts are worked. There are 9 (11) heel sts.

Heel Gussets

Knit 9 (11) heel sts, pick up and knit 13 (14) chain sts along right side of heel flap. Work 25 (28) instep sts in established pattern. With an empty needle, pick up and knit 13 (14) chain sts along left side of heel flap, knit 4 (5) sts from heel needle. There are 18 (20) sts on needle #1, 12 (14) sts on needle #2, 13 (14) sts on needle #3, and 17 (19) sts on needle #4.

Round 1: Work to 3 sts from end of needle #1, k2tog, k1. Work instep sts in established pattern. K1, ssk at beginning of needle #4, work to end.

Round 2: Work even in established pattern.

Repeat the last 2 rounds until there are 13 (14) sts on needle #1, 12 (14) sts on needle #2, 13 (14) sts on needle #3, and 12 (13) sts on needle #4. 50 (55) sts total.

FOOT

Continue even in stockinette stitch with MC for 4 (6) rounds. Work foot chart for 17 rounds.

Next Round: K2tog at end of needle #2 and beginning of needle #4 (increase 1 st at beginning of needle #4). Continue in stockinette stitch on these 48 (56) sts with MC until foot measures 2 (2½) inches (5 [6.5] cm) less than desired finished length.

Shape Toe

Round 1: *Work to last 2 sts on needle, k2tog; repeat from *.

Round 2: Work even.

Repeat the last 2 rounds until there are 6 (7) sts on each needle. Now work Round 1 (the decrease round) only until there are 8 sts remaining, 2 sts on each needle. Break yarn, thread tail through remaining sts, pull snug, and fasten off.

FINISHING

Weave in all ends. Block under a damp towel or on sock blockers.

Foot

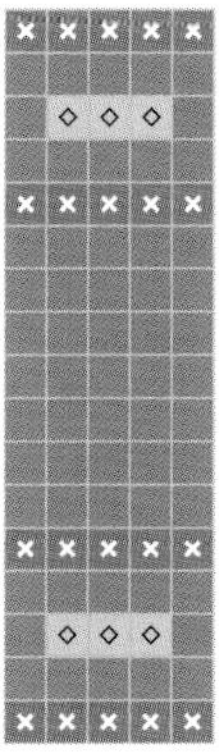

Leg

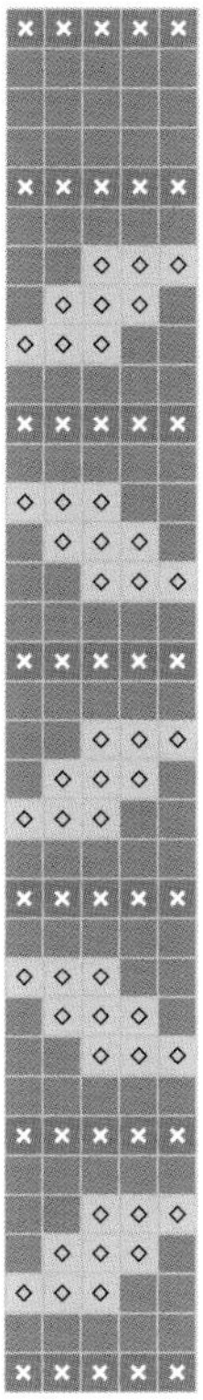

buckskin (MC)

rabbit brush (CC1)

turquoise (CC2)

SPEY VALLEY

The Spey Valley runs through the center of Scotland, north of Sterling. This is a place famous for *uisge beatha*, the water of life; whisky, single malt, scotch. It is the water in this valley that makes the drink so special and the stories and songs of hidden stills in lonely glens and rowdy Scotsmen in kilts add to the flavor. But this design was inspired by more than whisky—the yarn is tweedy and reminds me of socks I bought in a small shop in the Scottish border country years ago. The lateral braids around the sock leg are reminders of the rings around a barrel or whisky cask.

YARN

St. Ives (80% wool, 20% nylon, 197 yd [180 m]/50 g): #3104 Grouse, 2 skeins.

NEEDLES

Set of five double-pointed needles, size 0 (2 mm) or size needed to obtain correct gauge.

GAUGE

16 sts and 23 rounds = 2 inches (5 cm) in circular stockinette st before blocking.

FINISHED SIZE

About 7 inches (18 cm) around foot and 9½ inches (24 cm) from top of leg to bottom of heel.

Rib #1
Round 1: *P2, k2, p1, k2; repeat from *.

Repeat Round 1 for pattern.

Rib #2
Round 1: *P2, k5; repeat from *.

Round 2: *P2, k2, p1, k2; repeat from *.

Round 3: *P2, [k1, p1] twice, k1; repeat from *.

Round 4: Repeat Round 2.

Repeat Rounds 1–4 for pattern.

Rib #3
Round 1: *P2, k5; repeat from *.

Repeat Round 1 for pattern.

LEG

Cast on 63 sts. Divide sts onto 3 needles, 15 sts on needles #1 and #2, 33 sts on needle #3. Join into a round, being careful not to twist sts. This join is the "seam" line and marks the beginning of all future rounds. ***Note:*** The seam line is at the side of the leg, not the center back. Work 12 rounds of Rib #1.

Next Round: Work 1 round of Vikkel Braid.

Work 5 repeats of Rib #2 (20 rounds total).

Next Round: Work 1 round of Vikkel Braid.

Work Rib #3 until leg measures 7¾ inches (19.5 cm) or desired length to top of heel.

HEEL

Heel Flap

Work sl 1, k1 over 15 sts on needle #1 and 15 sts on needle #2, turn. P30, turn. These 30 sts form the heel flap. The remaining 33 sts will be held for the instep.

Row 1: *Sl 1, k1; repeat from *.

Row 2: Sl 1, p29.

Repeat the last 2 rows 14 more times for a total of 15 chain sts (see page 9) at each edge of heel flap.

Turn Heel

Row 1: Sl 1, k16, ssk, k1, turn.

Row 2: Sl 1, p5, p2tog, p1, turn.

Row 3: Sl 1, knit to within one st of the gap, ssk, k1, turn.

Row 4: Sl 1, purl to within one st of the gap, p2tog, p1, turn.

Repeat Rows 3 and 4 until all heel sts are worked. There are 18 heel sts.

Vikkel Braid

Vikkel is the Estonian word to describe patterns made with stitches that cross over each other. They are not cable stitches, where stitches cross with the use of an extra needle, but rather stitches that cross by knitting them "out of order." I named this type of lateral braid Vikkel because it is worked in this manner.

Increase one stitch by picking up the bar between the last stitch worked and the next stitch and knit it through the back loop. Place this stitch onto the left needle. *Bring the right needle behind this stitch, knit the next stitch through the back loop (figure 1), then knit the first stitch through the front as usual, and slip both stitches off (figure 2). Place the stitch just made onto the left needle (figure 3), and repeat from *. Remember to always drop both stitches after they are worked. At the end of the round, slip the first stitch back to the end of the last needle and pass the last stitch over the first stitch (as to bind off) then replace the first stitch on the left needle.

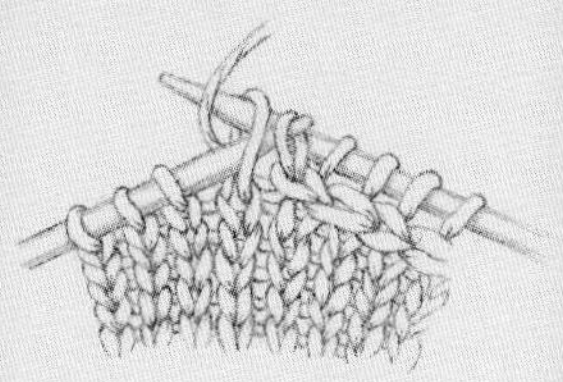
1

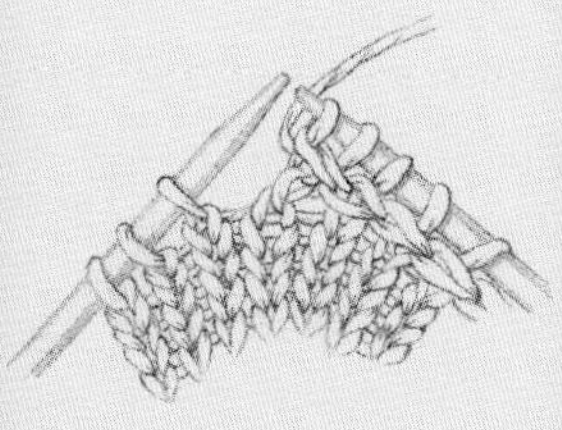
2

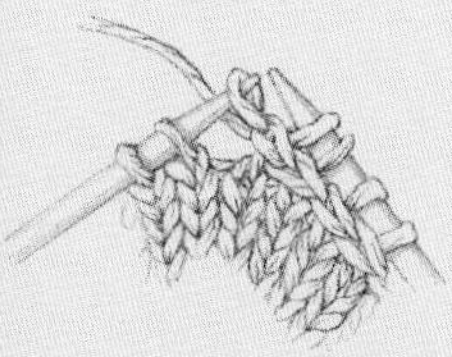
3

Heel Gussets

Knit 18 heel sts, pick up and knit 15 chain sts along right side of heel flap. Work 33 instep sts in established pattern. With an empty needle, pick up and knit 15 chain sts along left side of heel flap, knit 9 sts from heel needle. There are 24 sts on needles #1 and #3, 33 sts on needle #2.

Round 1: Work to 3 sts from end of needle #1, k2tog, k1. Work instep sts in established pattern. K1, ssk at beginning of needle #3, work to end.

Round 2: Work even in established pattern.

Repeat the last 2 rounds until there are 15 sts on needles #1 and #3. 63 sts total.

FOOT

Continue even in established pattern until foot measures 2½ inches (6.5 cm) less than desired finished length. Discontinue rib pattern. Adjust sts onto 4 needles (16 sts on needles #1, #2, and #3, 15 sts on needle #4).

Shape Toe

First Decrease Round: *K6, k2tog; repeat from *, ending k7.

Knit 6 rounds even.

Second Decrease Round: *K5, k2tog; rep from *.

Work 5 rounds even.

Third Decrease Round: *K4, k2tog; repeat from *.

Work 4 rounds even.

Fourth Decrease Round: *K3, k2tog; repeat from *.

Work 3 rounds even.

Fifth Decrease Round: *K2, k2tog; repeat from *.

Work 2 rounds even.

Sixth Decrease Round: *K1, k2 tog; repeat from *.

Work 1 round even.

Seventh Decrease Round: *K2tog; repeat from *.

8 sts remain, 2 sts on each needle. Break yarn, thread tail through remaining sts, pull snug, and fasten off.

FINISHING

Weave in all ends. Block under a damp towel or on sock blockers.

ALTERNATE HEEL

Square or Dutch Heel

Turn Heel

Row 1: Sl 1, k18, ssk, turn.

Row 2: Sl 1, p8, p2tog, turn.

Row 3: Sl 1, k8, ssk, turn.

Row 4: Sl 1, p8, p2tog, turn.

Repeat these last 2 rows until you have worked all the heel sts. There are 10 heel sts.

Heel Gussets

Knit 10 heel sts, pick up and knit 15 chain sts along right side of heel flap. Work 33 instep sts in established pattern. With an empty needle, pick up and knit 15 chain sts along left side of heel flap, knit 5 sts from heel needle. There are 20 sts on needles #1 and #4, 33 sts on needle #2.

Round 1: Work to 3 sts from end of needle #1, k2 tog, k1. Work instep sts in established pattern. K1, ssk at beginning of needle #3, work to end.

Round 2: Work even in established pattern.

Repeat the last 2 rounds until there are 15 sts on needles #1 and #3. 63 sts remain.

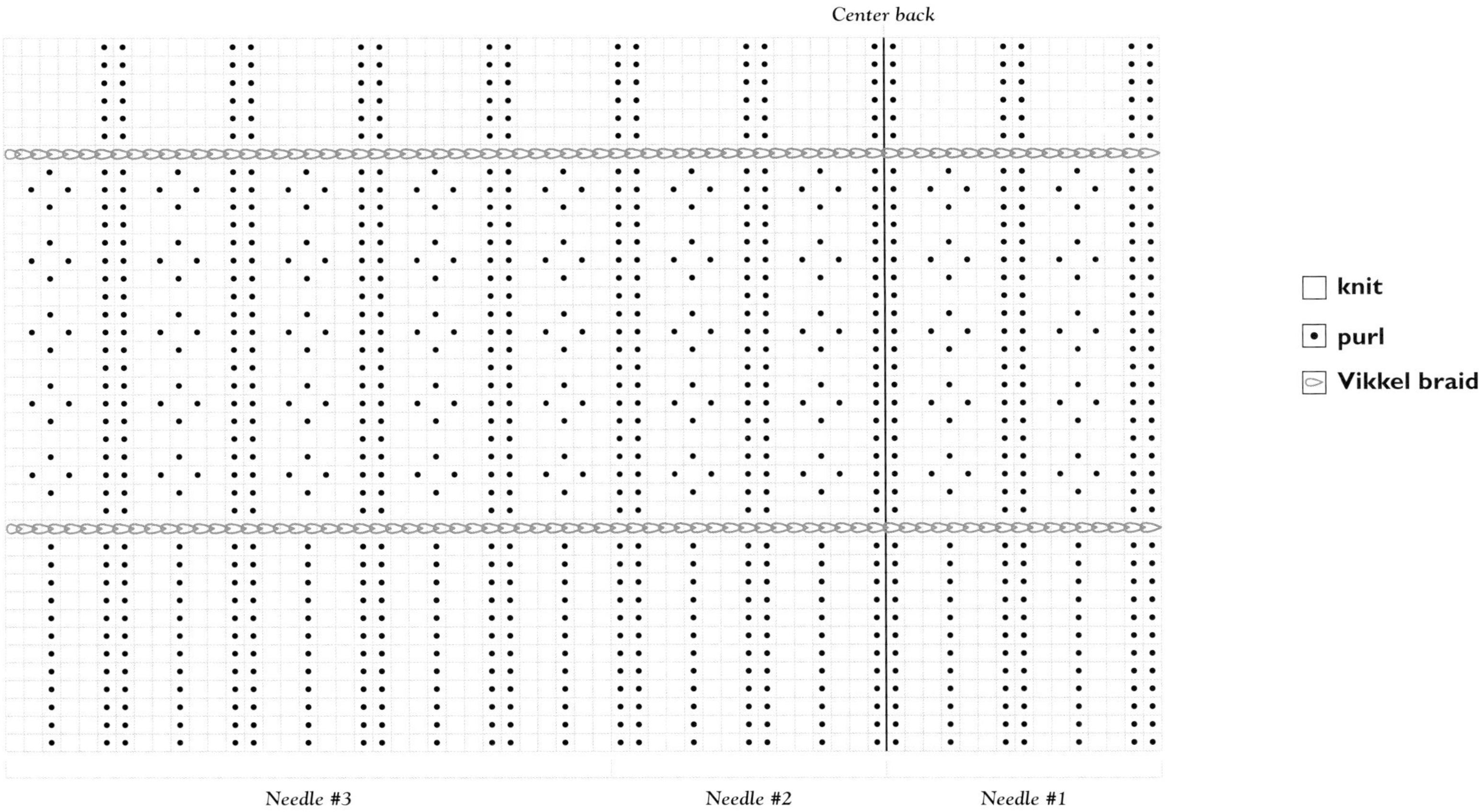

Center back
Needle #3
Needle #2
Needle #1
knit
purl
Vikkel braid

STRUMP

CHRISTMAS IN TALLINN

Tallinn, Estonia, is one of the most special cities I have ever experienced. I have been there in spring, in autumn, and in summer, but never at Christmastime. This remains a great dream of mine, to spend Christmas in Tallinn, to see the snow falling on the cobblestones, candles shining out into the darkness of a winter's day, and to hear Estonian carols sung by beautiful voices. This sock design brings me closer to the dream. I used traditional Estonian patterning on the leg, and included Estonian-inspired designs at the cuff. The non-traditional foot will hold lots of goodies.

YARN

Dale of Norway Tiur (60% mohair, 40% wool, 126 yd [115 m]/50 g): #4136 red, #0020 natural, and #7562 dark green, 1 skein each.

NEEDLES

Set of five double-pointed needles size 3 (3.25 mm) and size 2 (2.75 mm) or size needed to obtain correct gauge.

GAUGE

12 sts and 14 rounds = 2 inches (5 cm) in circular, patterned stockinette stitch on larger needles before blocking.

FINISHED SIZE

About 12 inches (30.5 cm) around leg and 12 inches (30.5 cm) from top of leg to bottom of heel.

Note: Leave long tails when casting on and when starting a new color near the top of the sock so you can use the tails later for making the braided loop.

LEG

With green and larger needle, cast on 92 sts, using the Double-start Cast-on (see page 7) over one needle only. Divide sts onto 4 needles (23 sts on each needle). Join into a round, being careful not to twist sts. This join is the "seam" line and marks the beginning of all future rounds. Work Kihnu Vits as described on page 75 using red and natural.

Begin Cuff chart as indicated. When Cuff chart is complete, work 2 rounds of Kihnu Vits again, using green and natural.

Follow leg chart, decreasing 2 sts (1 at end of needle #1 and 1 at beginning of needle #4) on first round of chart (a solid red round). 90 sts remain. Work until leg measures 10½ inches (26.5 cm) and you have completed 3 repeats of the Star pattern and the 4-round border as shown on chart.

Next Round: Decrease 8 stitches evenly. 82 sts remain.

Adjust stitches so there are 17 sts on needles #1 and #4, 24 sts on needles #2 and #3. Change to smaller needles.

HEEL

Heel Flap

Knit 17 sts on needle #1, turn. P34, turn. These 34 sts form the heel flap. The remaining 48 sts will be held for the instep.

Row 1: *Sl 1, k33; repeat from *.

Row 2: *Sl 1, p33; repeat from *.

Repeat the last 2 rows 7 more times for a total of 8 chain sts (see page 9) at each edge of heel flap.

Turn Heel

Row 1: Sl 1, k18, ssk, k1, turn.

Row 2: Sl 1, p5, p2tog, p1, turn.

Row 3: Sl 1, knit to within one st of the gap, ssk, k1, turn.

Row 4: Sl 1, purl to within one st of the gap, p2tog, p1, turn.

Repeat Rows 3 and 4 until all heel sts are worked. There are 20 heel sts.

Kihnu Vits

Kihnu is an Estonian island, home of wonderful knitting traditions. *Vits* in Estonian means hoop or band, and also describes the bands that encircle wooden beer mugs, made like cooper's barrels. In this case, it is a band that circles the leg of a sock.

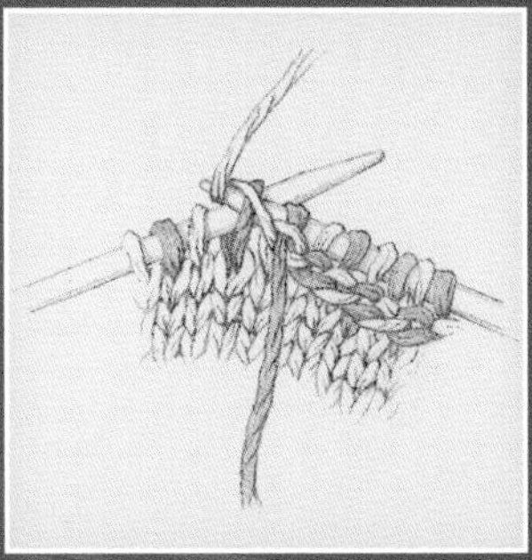

Round 1: *K1 CC, k1 MC; repeat from *.

Round 2: Bring both colors to the front as if to purl, *purl the CC st with MC and purl the MC st with CC, bringing each color *under* the other every time you change. Repeat from *

Heel Gussets

Knit 20 heel sts, pick up and knit 8 chain sts along right side of heel flap. Work 48 instep sts. With an empty needle, pick up and knit 8 chain sts along left side of heel flap, knit 10 sts from heel needle. There are 18 sts on needles #1 and #4, 24 sts on needles #2 and #3.

Round 1: Work to 3 sts from end of needle #1, k2tog, k1. Work instep sts in stockinette stitch. K1, ssk at beginning of needle #4, work to end.

Round 2: Work even in stockinette stitch.

Repeat the last 2 rounds once more. There are 16 sts on needles #1 and #4. 80 sts total.

FOOT

Continue even until foot measures 2½ inches (6.5 cm). Adjust sts so there are 20 sts on each needle.

Shape Toe

First Decrease Round: *K6, k2tog; repeat from *.

Work 6 rounds even.

Second Decrease Round: *K5, k2tog; repeat from *.

Work 5 rounds even.

Third Decrease Round: *K4, k2tog; repeat from *.

Work 4 rounds even.

Fourth Decrease Round: *K3, k2tog; repeat from *.

Work 3 rounds even.

Fifth Decrease Round: *K2, k2tog; repeat from *.

Work 2 rounds even.

Sixth Decrease Round: *K1, k2tog; repeat from *.

Work 1 round even.

Seventh Decrease Round: *K2tog; repeat from *.

There are 10 sts remaining. Break yarn, thread tail through remaining sts, pull snug, and fasten off.

FINISHING

Using tails that remain at the cuff, adding more threads where needed, make a braid as follows: Divide into 3 groups of 3 threads each, 1 of each color. Braid the threads into a piece about 4 inches (10 cm) long. Secure them by making an overhand knot at the end. Loop this braid back toward the top of the cuff and attach it securely inside the cuff edge. Weave in all ends. Block under a damp towel.

red

natural

dark green

• purl with appropriate color

Work twice

Cuff

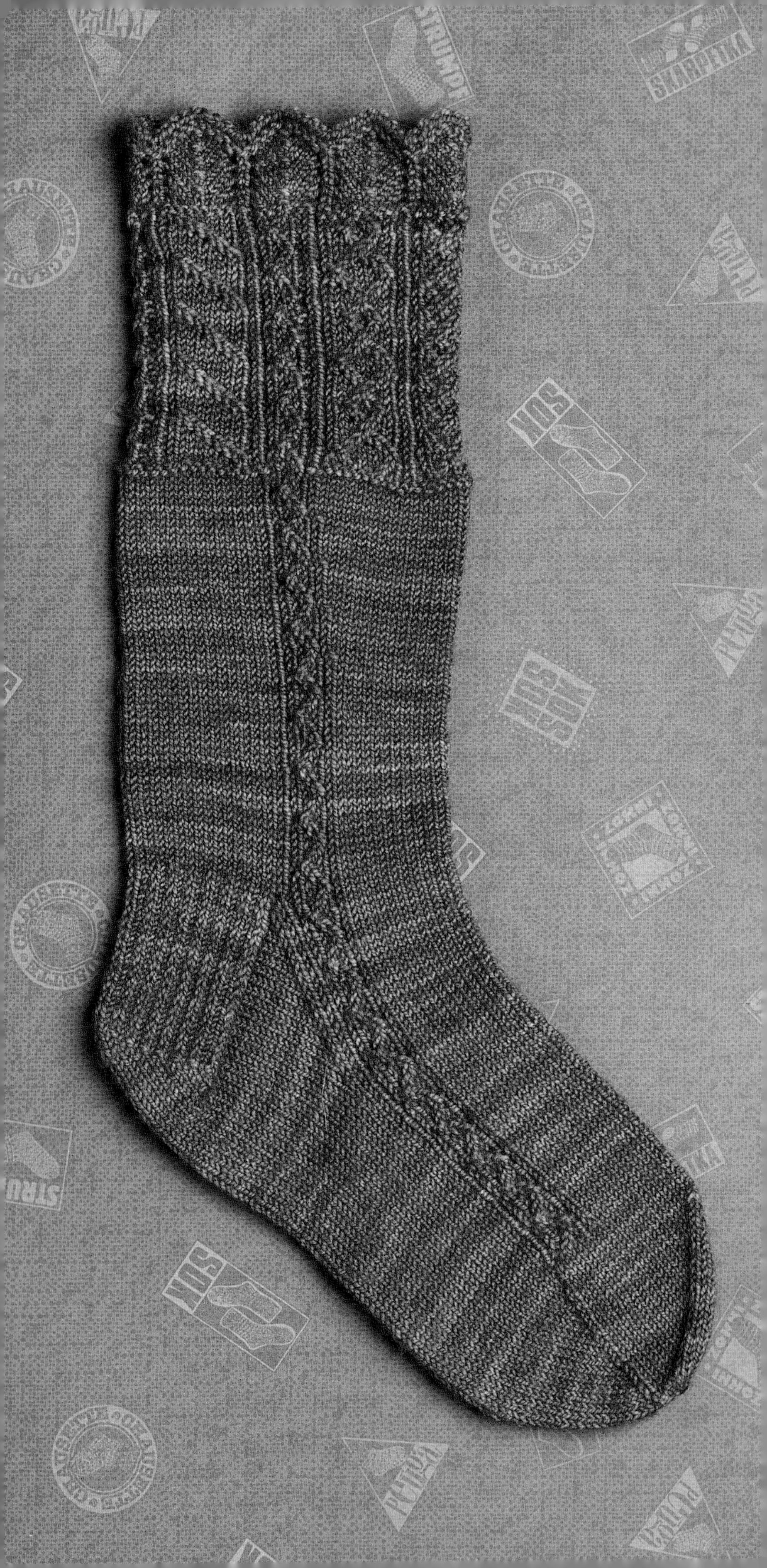

TRAVELER'S STOCKINGS

The idea for this stocking design came to me while I was traveling and researching the knitting of Estonia. Among the many beautiful knitted items I saw was a wonderful pair of stockings decorated with a collection of intricate designs. I was fascinated by the stockings and I thought of them many times after my trip had ended, remembering their beauty. This design was born during my travels and the seemingly complex patterns used are composed of simple-to-make traveling stitches. This design is an excellent one to work during a journey—once the design is set up, it is easy to follow.

YARN

Koigu Premium Merino (100% wool; 176 yd [161 m]/50 g): #2128 Mauve, 3 skeins.

NEEDLES

Set of five double-pointed needles size 0 (2 mm) or size needed to obtain the correct gauge.

GAUGE

18 sts and 28 rounds = 2 inches (5 cm) in circular stockinette stitch before blocking.

FINISHED SIZE

About 7½ inches (19 cm) around foot and 10 inches (25.5 cm) from top of leg to bottom of heel.

LEG

Cast on 80 sts. Divide sts evenly onto 4 needles (20 sts on each needle). Using the crossover method (see page 7), join into a round being careful not to twist sts. This join is the "seam" line and marks the beginning of all future rounds. ***Note:*** The seam line is at the side of the leg, not the center back. Knit 1 round. Purl 1 round. Knit 1 round.

Work Lacy Cuff Pattern

Round 1: *K1, yo, k3, sl 1, k2tog, psso, k3, yo; repeat from *.

Round 2: Knit.

Work Rounds 1 and 2 four more times, for a total of 10 rounds.

Note: Because you are ending the pattern rounds with a yo, always complete Round 2 (a knit round) before putting your work down so you won't lose the last yo.

Purl 1 round, decrease 2 sts evenly spaced—78 sts remain. Adjust sts on needles so there are 17 sts on needles #1 and #2 and 22 sts on needles #3 and #4. Work Chart 1 as indicated, purling the last round and keeping clock patterns at beginning of needle #3 and end of needle #4 as established.

Shape Leg

Begin Chart 2. Knit 1 round, keeping clock patterns as established.

Decrease Round: K34, p1, pattern over 4 sts, p1, ssk, k28, k2tog, p1, pattern over 4 sts, p1—2 sts decreased.

Continue working stockinette stitch and clocks as established and shown on chart and *at the same time* on every sixth round of clock pattern work shaping decreases on needles #3 and #4 (see chart 2). Repeat this decrease 4 more times—5 times total. 68 sts remain.

Continue in stockinette stitch, keeping clock pattern as established, until leg measures 8¼ inches (21 cm) or desired length to top of heel.

HEEL

Heel Flap

Knit 17 sts on needles #1 and 17 sts on #2 onto one needle, turn. P34, turn. These 34 sts form the heel flap. The remaining 34 sts will be held for the instep.

Row 1: *Sl 1, k1; repeat from *, turn.

Row 2: Sl 1, p33.

Repeat the last 2 rows 16 more times for a total of 17 chain sts (see page 9) at each edge of heel flap.

Turn Heel

Row 1: Sl 1, k18, ssk, k1, turn.

Row 2: Sl 1, p5, p2tog, p1, turn.

Row 3: Sl 1, knit to 1 st from gap, ssk, k1, turn.

Row 4: Sl 1, purl to 1 st from gap, p2tog, p1, turn.

Repeat Rows 3 and 4 until all heel sts have been worked. There are 20 heel sts.

Heel Gussets

Knit 20 heel sts, pick up and knit 17 chain sts along right side of heel flap. Work 34 instep sts in established pattern. With an empty needle, pick up and knit 17 chain sts along left side of heel flap, knit 10 sts from heel needle. There are 27 sts on needles #1 and #4, and 17 sts on needles #2 and #3.

Round 1: Work to 3 sts from end of needle #1, k2tog, k1. Work instep sts in established pattern. K1, ssk at beginning of needle #4, work to end.

Round 2: Work even in established pattern.

Repeat the last 2 rounds until there are 17 sts on each needle. 68 sts total.

FOOT

Continue even in established pattern until foot measures 2 inches (5 cm) less than desired finished length. Discontinue clock pattern and continue in stockinette stitch.

Shape Toe

Round 1: *Work to last 2 sts on needle, k2tog; repeat from * to end.

Round 2: Work even.

Repeat the last 2 rounds until there are 8 sts on each needle. Work Round 1 (the decrease round) only until there are 8 sts remaining, 2 sts on each needle.

Break yarn, thread tail through remaining sts, pull snug, and fasten off.

FINISHING

Weave in all ends. Block under a damp towel or on sock blockers.

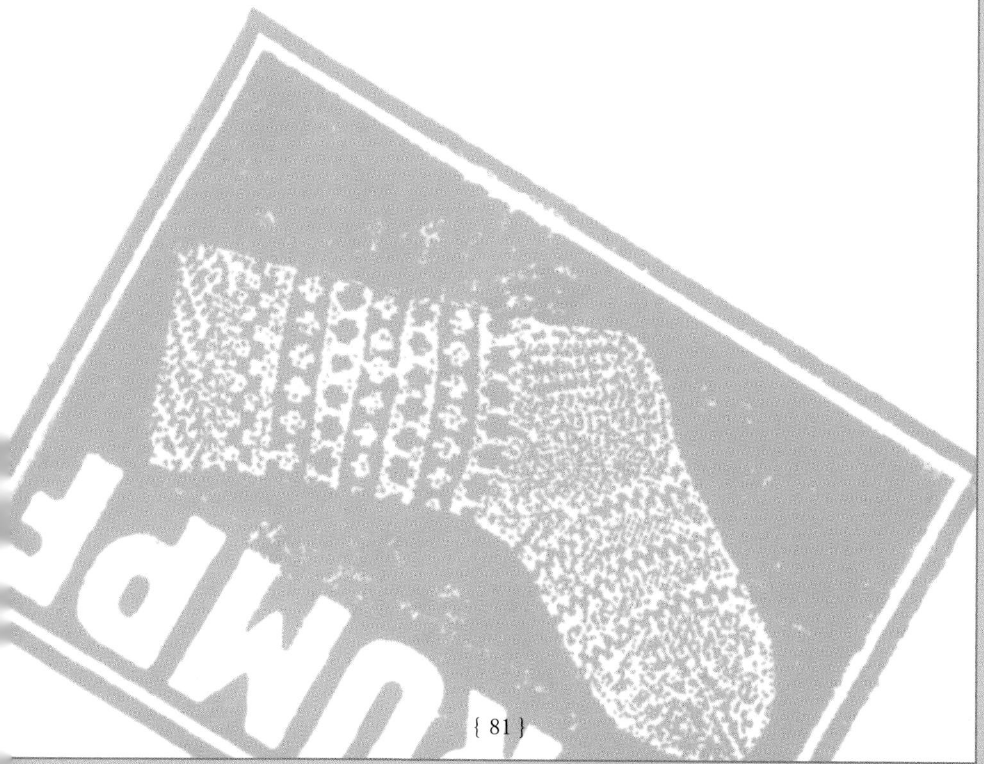

Traveler's - chart 2

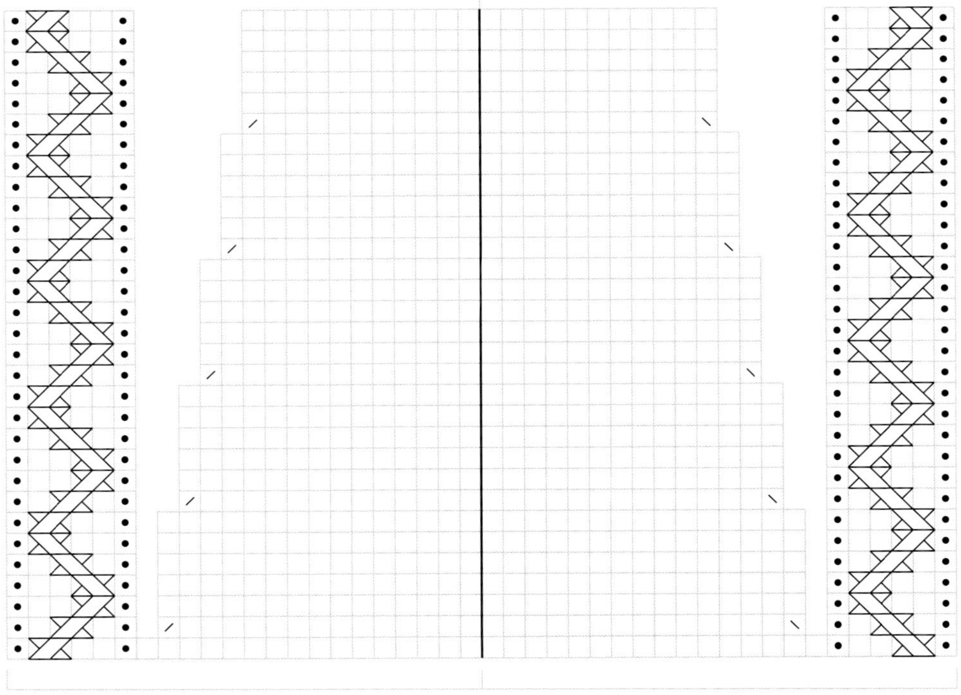

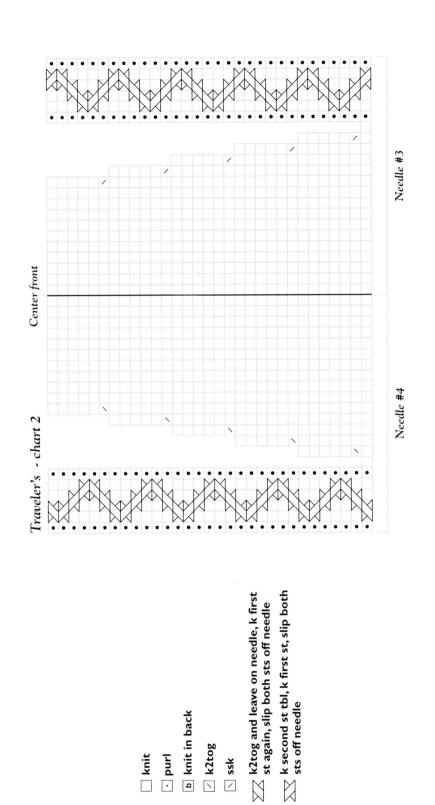

- knit
- · purl
- b knit in back
- k2tog
- ssk
- k2tog and leave on needle, k first st again, slip both sts off needle
- k second st tbl, k first st, slip both sts off needle

Traveler's - chart 1

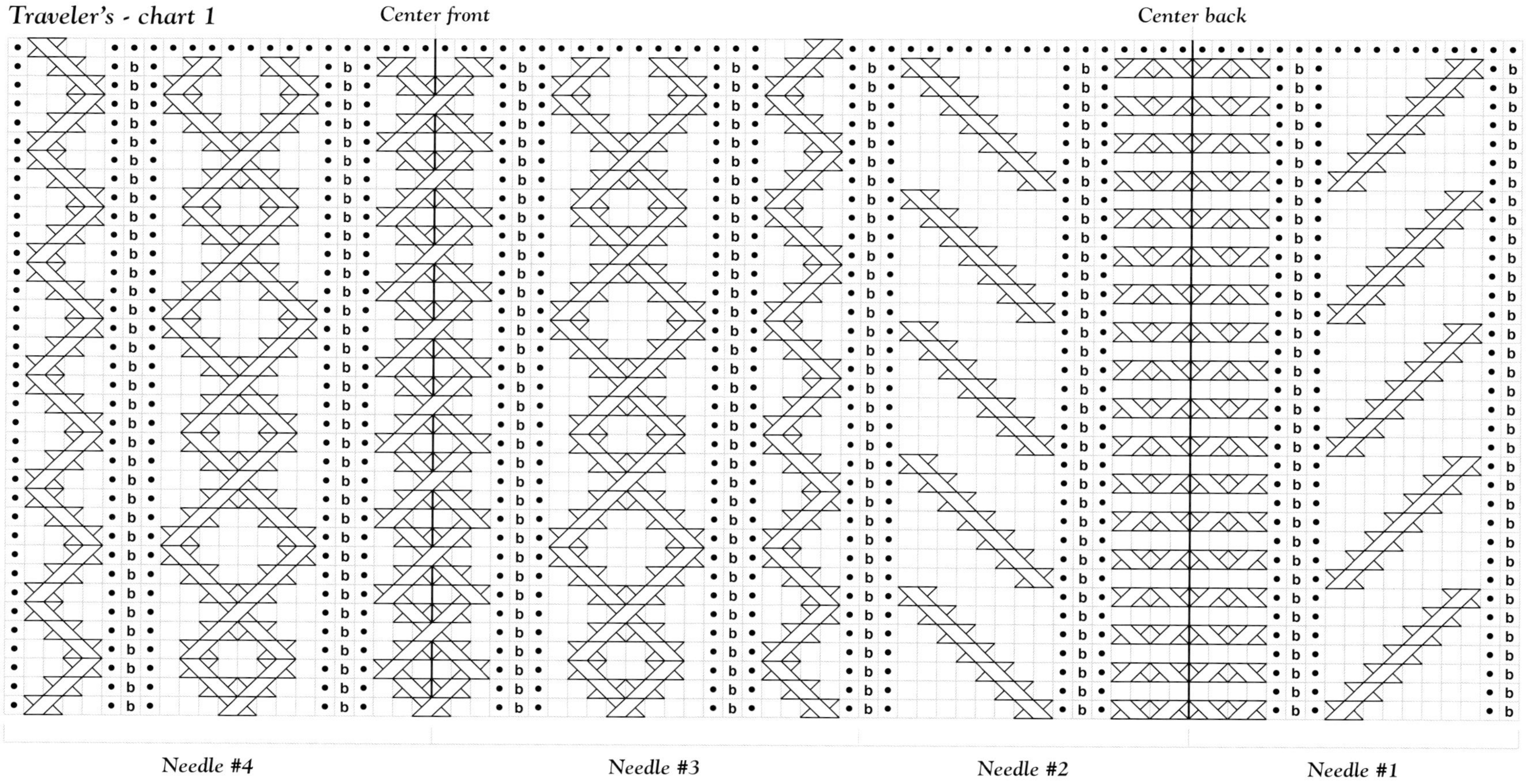

UINTA CABIN

The color of these socks reflects the landscape near our cabin in the foothills of the Uinta Mountains in Eastern Utah. This remote spot provides a secluded haven for weekend getaways, and it is complete with a spectacular view of a valley with a stream and distant ranch land. The patterns on these socks are taken from ranch brand or logo designs, a common sight in the West, where you'll pass a gate or roadway with the name of the ranch and its "brand" prominently displayed. I enjoy traveling around this landscape; I take my knitting, while my sweetheart does the fishing.

YARN

Happy Trails Sock Yarn (90% wool, 10% nylon, 132 yards [120 m]/50 g): Sagebrush (MC), 2 skeins; Rabbit Brush (CC1), Pinon (CC2), and Fleece (CC3), 1 skein each.

NEEDLES

Set of five double-pointed needles size 3 (3.25 mm) or size needed to obtain the correct gauge.

GAUGE

12 sts and 14 rounds = 2 inches (5 cm) in circular stockinette stitch before blocking.

FINISHED SIZE

About 8½ inches (21.5 cm) around foot and 9½ inches (24 cm) from top of leg to bottom of heel.

Note: Increase in next st by knitting into the front of the stitch and then knitting into the back of the same stitch.

LEG

With CC2, cast on 54 sts. Divide sts onto 4 needles, (12 sts on needles #1, #2, and #3 and 18 sts on needle #4). Join into a round, being careful not to twist sts. This join is the "seam" line and marks the beginning of all future rounds. Purl 1 round.

Next round: *K2, increase in next st, k2, k2tog; repeat from *.

Repeat the last round 2 more times. Change to MC and repeat last round 3 times. Change to CC1 and repeat last round 3 times.

Continue in stockinette stitch, following chart as indicated and increasing 1 st on Rounds 17 and 23. Adjust sts so there are 14 sts on each needle. The seam line is at the center back, between needles #1 and #4. Work to end of leg chart, ending last round ready to begin needle #4.

HEEL

Heel Flap

Begin with first st on needle #4. With CC2, knit 14 sts on needle #4 and 14 sts on needle #1 onto one needle, turn. P28, turn. These 28 sts form the heel flap. The remaining 28 sts will be held for the instep.

Row 1: *Sl 1, k1; repeat from *.

Row 2: Sl 1, p27.

Repeat the last 2 rows 13 more times for a total of 14 chain sts (see page 9) at each edge of heel flap.

Turn Heel

Row 1: Sl 1, k15, ssk, k1, turn.

Row 2: Sl 1, p5, p2tog, p1, turn.

Row 3: Sl 1, knit to within one st of the gap, ssk, k1, turn.

Row 4: Sl 1, purl to within one st of the gap, p2tog, p1, turn.

Repeat Rows 3 and 4 until all heel sts are worked, ending last repeat of Row 3 with the ssk, and last repeat of Row 4 with the p2tog. There are 16 heel sts.

Heel Gussets

Continuing with CC2, knit 16 heel sts, pick up and knit 14 chain sts along right side of heel flap. Work 28 instep sts. With an empty needle, pick up and knit 14 chain sts along left side of heel flap, knit 8 sts from heel needle. There are 22 sts on needles #1 and #4, 14 sts on needles #2 and #3.

Round 1: Change to CC1 and CC3 and follow foot chart. Work to 3 sts from end of needle #1, k2tog, k1. Work instep sts in established pattern. K1, ssk at beginning of needle #4, work to end.

Round 2: With CC2, work even.

Continuing with MC, repeat the last 2 rounds until there are 14 sts on needles #1 and #3. 56 sts total.

FOOT

Continue in stockinette stitch until foot measures 3½ inches (9 cm) less than desired finished length. Knit one round with CC2. Knit one round alternating CC1 and CC3.

Shape Toe

Continue with CC2.

First Decrease Round: *K6, k2tog; repeat from *.

Knit 6 rounds even.

Second Decrease Round: *K5, k2tog; repeat from *.

Work 5 rounds even.

Third Decrease Round: *K4, k2tog; repeat from *.

Work 4 rounds even.

Fourth Decrease Round: *K3, k2tog; repeat from *.

Work 3 rounds even.

Fifth Decrease Round: *K2, k2tog; repeat from *.

Work 2 rounds even.

Sixth Decrease Round: *K1, k2tog; repeat from *.

Work 1 round even.

Seventh Decrease Round: *K2tog; repeat from *.

7 sts remain. Break yarn, thread tail through remaining sts, pull snug, and fasten off.

FINISHING

Weave in all ends. Block under a damp towel or on sock blockers.

Foot

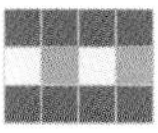

Leg

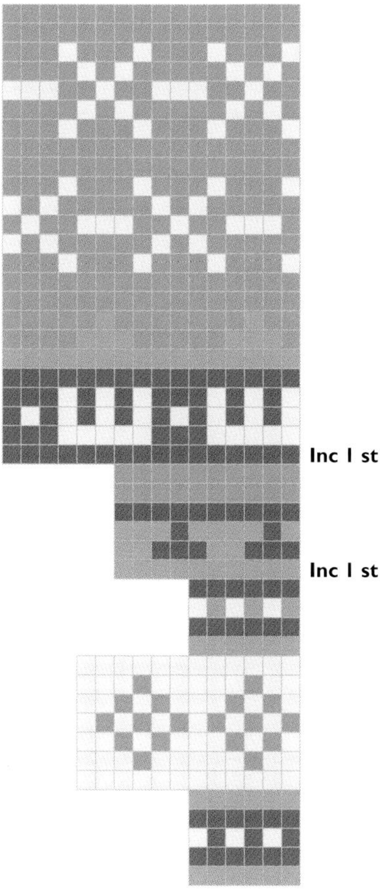

- sagebrush (MC)
- rabbit brush (CC1)
- pinon (CC2)
- fleece (CC3)

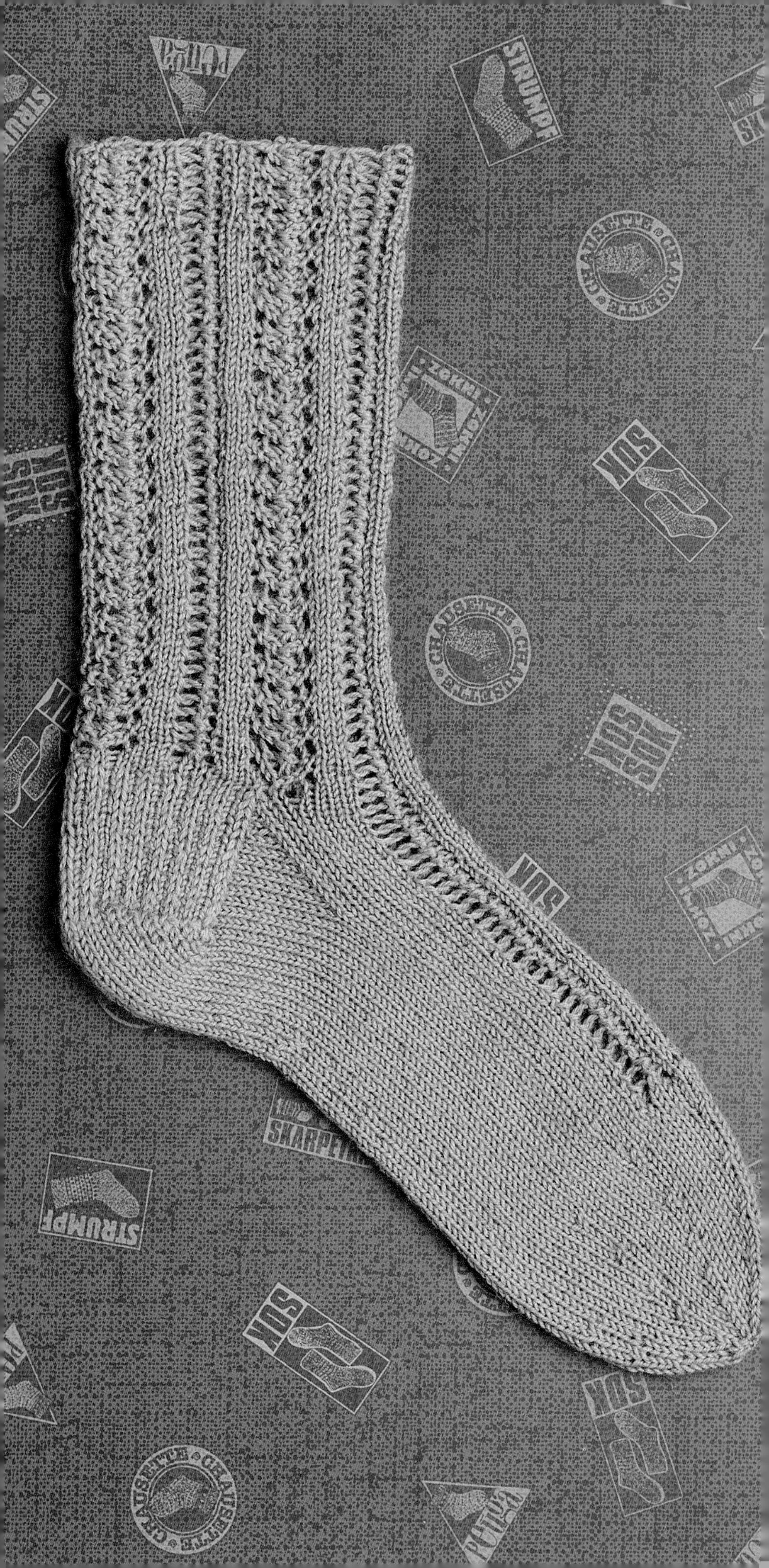
STRUMPF
SOK
STRUMPF

UNST

Unst is the northernmost Shetland Island. To get there you take a ferry from one island to the next and the ride is no longer than fifteen minutes. Unst is a beautiful place with small crofts dotting the landscape and sheep everywhere. Unst is famous for lace knitting and known for finely knitted shawls that decorated the wealthy women of Europe in the nineteenth and early twentieth centuries. The knitting also inspired hundreds of knitters in our own time. Here I used the Shetland lace pattern called Columns and Arches—it has a nice stripe effect, which I think suits the shape of a sock.

YARN

Lang JaWoll (75% wool, 18% nylon, 7% acrylic, 206 yd [188 m]/50 g): #8392 Light Green, 2 skeins.

NEEDLES

Set of five double-pointed needles size 1 (2.25 mm) or size needed to obtain correct gauge.

GAUGE

16 sts and 20 rounds = 2 inches (5 cm) in circular stockinette stitch before blocking.

FINISHED SIZE

About 7½ inches (19 cm) around foot and 8½ inches (21.5 cm) from top of leg to bottom of heel.

COLUMNS AND ARCHES

***Rounds 1 and 3:* Knit.**

***Round 2:* *K1, yo, k1, sl 1, k2tog, psso, k1, yo, k3, yo, sl 1, k2tog, psso, yo, k2; repeat from *.**

***Round 4:* *K2, yo, sl 1, k2tog, psso, yo, k4, yo, sl 1, k2tog, psso, yo, k2; repeat from *.**

Repeat Rounds 1–4 for pattern.

LEG

Cast on 56 sts. Divide sts evenly onto 4 needles (14 sts on each needle). Join into a round, being careful not to twist sts. This join is the "seam" line and marks the beginning of all future rounds.

Rounds 1 and 3: *K7, p1, k5, p1; repeat from *.

Round 2: *K1, yo, k1, sl 1, k2tog, psso, k1, yo, k1, p1, k1, yo, sl 1, k2tog, psso, yo, k1, p1; repeat from *.

Round 4: *K2, yo, sl 1, k2tog, psso, yo, k2, p1, k1, yo, sl 1, k2tog, psso, yo, k1, p1; repeat from *.

Repeat Rounds 1–4 for 12 rounds total. Rib is complete.

Continue working Columns and Arches pattern until leg measures 7 inches (18 cm) or desired length to top of heel, ending having completed Round 4 of pattern and knitting the last 2 sts tog. 55 sts remain. Adjust sts so there are 18 sts on needle #1, 10 sts on needle #2, 17 sts on needle #3, and 10 sts on needle #4.

HEEL

Heel Flap

Knit 18 sts on needle #1, turn. P28, turn. These 28 sts form the heel flap. The remaining 27 sts will be held for the instep.

Row 1: *Sl 1, k1; repeat from *.

Row 2: Sl 1, p27.

Repeat the last 2 rows 13 more times for a total 14 chain sts (see page 9) at each edge of heel flap.

Turn Heel

Row 1: Sl 1, k15, ssk, k1, turn.

Row 2: Sl 1, p5, p2tog, p1, turn.

Row 3: Sl 1, knit to within one st of the gap, ssk, k1, turn.

Row 4: Sl 1, purl to within one st of the gap, p2tog, p1, turn.

Repeat Rows 3 and 4 until all the heel sts are worked. There are 16 heel sts.

Heel Gussets

Knit 16 heel sts, pick up and knit 14 chain sts along right side of heel flap. Work 27 instep sts in established pattern onto needle #2, beginning with Round 1 of pattern. With an empty needle, pick up and knit 14 chain sts along left side of heel flap, knit 8 sts from heel needle. There are 22 sts on needles #1 and #3, 27 sts on needle #2.

Round 1: Work to 3 sts from the end of needle #1, k2tog, k1. Work instep sts in established pattern. K1, ssk at beginning of needle #3, work to end.

Round 2: Work even in established pattern.

Repeat the last 2 rounds until there are 14 sts on needles #1 and #3. 55 sts total.

FOOT

Continue even in established pattern until foot measures 3 inches (7.5 cm) less than desired finished length. Work stockinette stitch for 5 rounds.

Shape Toe

Adjust sts so there are 14 sts on needles #1, #2, and #3 and 13 sts on needle #4.

First Decrease Round: *K6, k2tog; repeat from *, ending k7.

Work 6 rounds even.

Second Decrease Round: *K5, k2tog; repeat from *.

Work 5 rounds even.

Third Decrease Round: *K4, k2tog; repeat from *.

Work 4 rounds even.

Fourth Decrease Round: *K3, k2tog; repeat from *.

Work 3 rounds even.

Fifth Decrease Round: *K2, k2tog; repeat from *.

Work 2 rounds even.

Sixth Decrease Round: *K1, k2tog; repeat from *.

Work 1 round even.

Seventh Decrease Round: *K2tog; repeat from *.

There are 7 toe sts. Break yarn, thread tail through remaining sts, pull snug, and fasten off.

FINISHING

Weave in all ends. Block under a damp towel or on sock blockers.

- ☐ **knit**
- ⊡ **purl**
- ◯ **yarn over**
- ∧ **Sl 1, k2tog, psso**

Foot

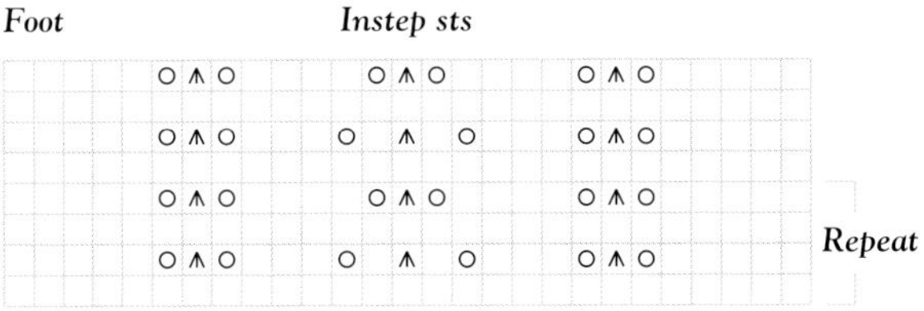

Leg

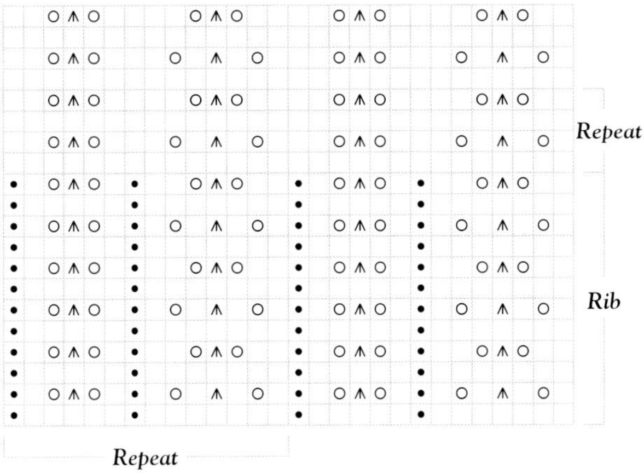

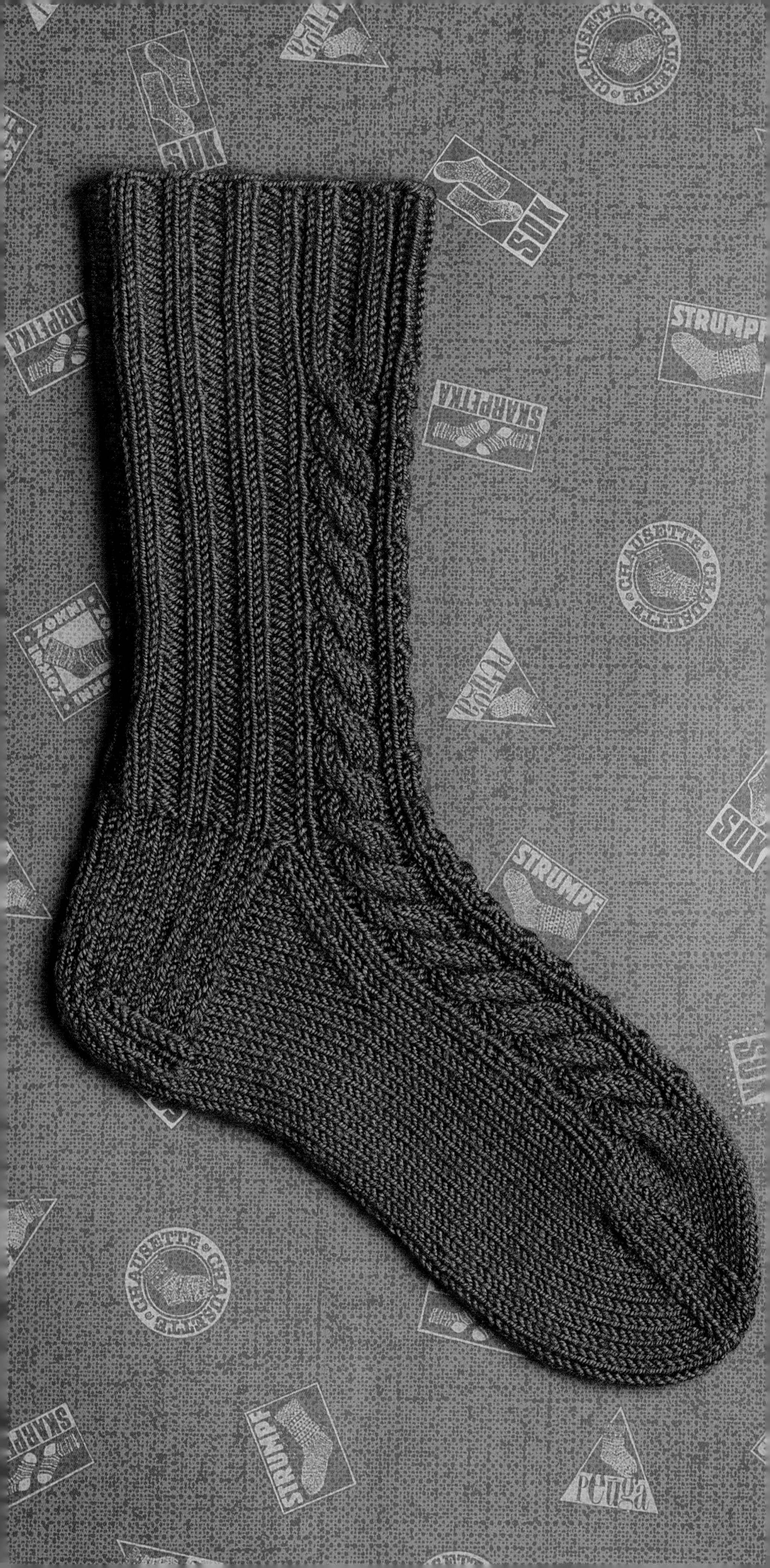
STRUMPF
SKARPETKA
SOK
CHAUSSETTE

WHITBY

Whitby is located on the east coast of Yorkshire, England. It is an ancient town with a colorful history of smugglers and fishermen and their wonderful gansy sweaters. I have wandered the winding streets of the old part of Whitby and enjoyed a visit to a yarn store housed in an old church. I have imagined what it must have been like when tall ships were at the docks and women in their shawls were knitting, waiting for the herring boats to arrive, when they would begin their long day's work. These socks are based on a pattern found on a sailor's gansy from Whitby.

YARN

Louet Gems (100% Merino wool, 225 yd [206 m]/100 g): 41 Antique Olive, 2 skeins.

NEEDLES

Set of five double-pointed needles size 2 (2.75 mm) or size needed to obtain correct gauge. Cable needle.

GAUGE

13 sts and 20 rounds = 2 inches (5 cm) in circular stockinette stitch before blocking.

FINISHED SIZE

About 7½ inches (19 cm) around foot and 9 inches (23 cm) from top of leg to bottom of heel.

STITCHES

Left Cable **Place 3 sts onto cable needle, hold in front of work, knit 3 sts, knit 3 sts from cable needle.**

Right Cable **Place 3 sts onto cable needle, hold in back of work, knit 3 sts, knit 3 sts from cable needle.**

LEG

Cast on 51 sts. Divide sts onto 3 needles (13 sts on needles #1 and #2, 25 sts on needle #3). Join into a round, being careful not to twist sts. This join is the "seam" line and marks the beginning of all future rounds. ***Note:*** The seam line is at the side of the leg, not the center back.

Work p2, k2 rib over needles #1 and #2 and follow chart for 25 center front/instep sts on needle #3. Work until leg measures 7¼ inches (18.5 cm) or desired length to top of heel.

HEEL

Heel Flap

*Sl 1, k1; repeat from * to end of needle #2, turn. P26, turn. These 26 sts form the heel flap. The remaining 25 sts will be held for the instep.

Row 1: *Sl 1, k1; repeat from *.

Row 2: Sl 1, p25.

Repeat the last 2 rows 16 more times for a total of 17 chain sts (see page 9) at each edge of heel flap.

Turn Heel

Row 1: Keeping in pattern, (sl 1, k1) over 16 sts, ssk, turn.

Row 2: Sl 1, p6, p2tog, turn.

Row 3: Sl 1, (sl 1, k1) 3 times, ssk, turn.

Row 4: Sl 1, p6, p2tog, turn.

Repeat Rows 3 and 4 until all heel sts are worked. There are 8 heel sts.

Heel Gussets

Knit 8 heel sts, pick up and knit 17 chain sts along right side of heel flap. Work 25 instep sts in established pattern. With an empty needle, pick up and knit 17 chain sts along left side of heel flap, knit 4 sts from heel needle. There are 21 sts on needles #1 and #3, 25 sts on needle #2.

Round 1: Work to 3 sts from end of needle #1, k2tog, k1. Work instep sts in established pattern. K1, ssk at beginning of needle #3, work to end.

Round 2: Work even in established pattern.

Repeat the last 2 rounds until there are 13 sts on needles #1 and #3. 51 sts total.

FOOT

Continue even in established pattern until there are 17 pattern repeats total or to desired length. End cable pattern having worked a cable cross round. Continue in stockinette stitch until foot measures 2 inches (5 cm) less than desired finished length.

Shape Toe
Adjust sts onto 4 needles (13 sts on needles #1, #2, and #4, 12 sts on needle #3).

Round 1: Work to within 3 sts from end of needle #1, k2tog, k1. K1, ssk at beginning of needle #2. Work to within 3 sts from end of needle #3, k2tog, k1. K1, ssk at beginning of needle #4, work to end.

Round 2: Work even.

Repeat the last 2 rounds until there are 7 sts on needles #1, #2, and #4, and 6 sts on needle #3. Work Round 1 (the decrease round) only until there are 3 sts on needles #1, #2, and #4. On next round, decrease only on these 3 needles. 8 sts remain, 2 sts on each needle.

Break yarn, thread tail through remaining sts, pull snug, and fasten off.

FINISHING

Weave in all ends. Block under a damp towel or on sock blockers.

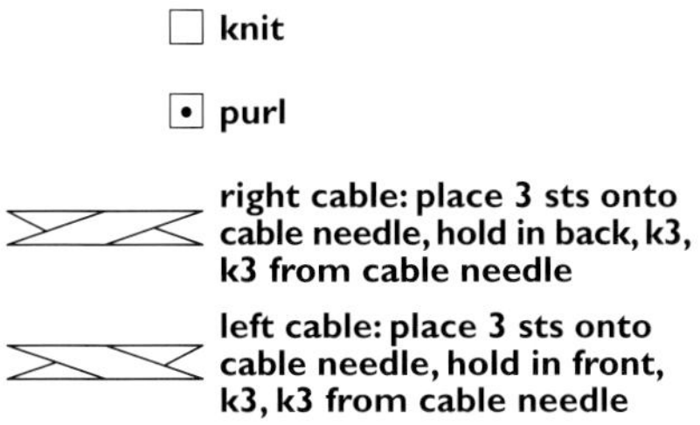

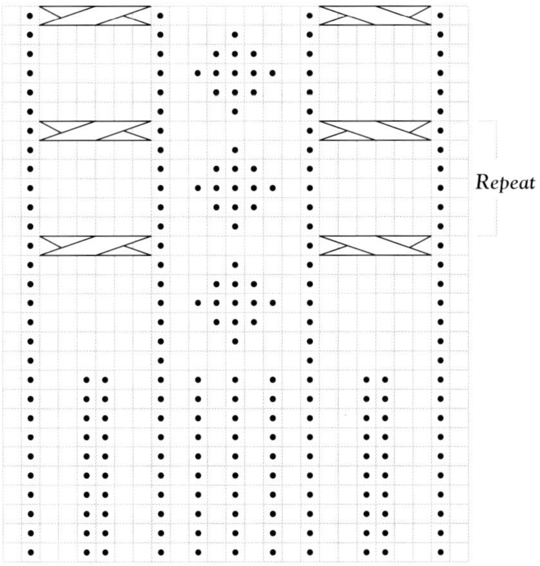

Center front/Instep sts

INDEX

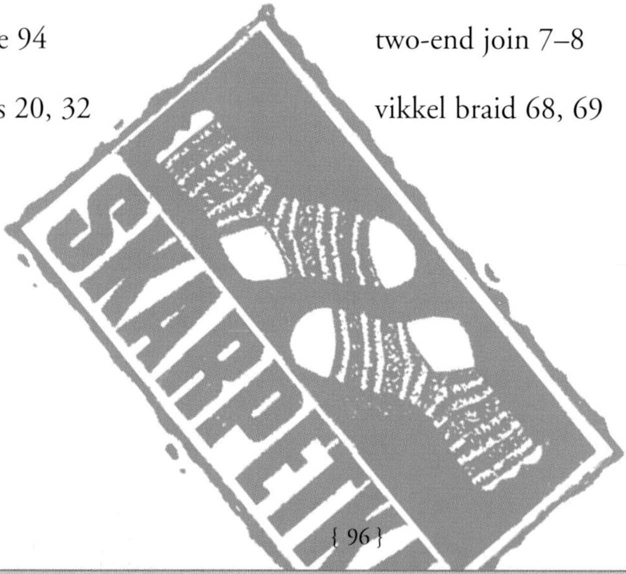